Insights

Ben Clayton

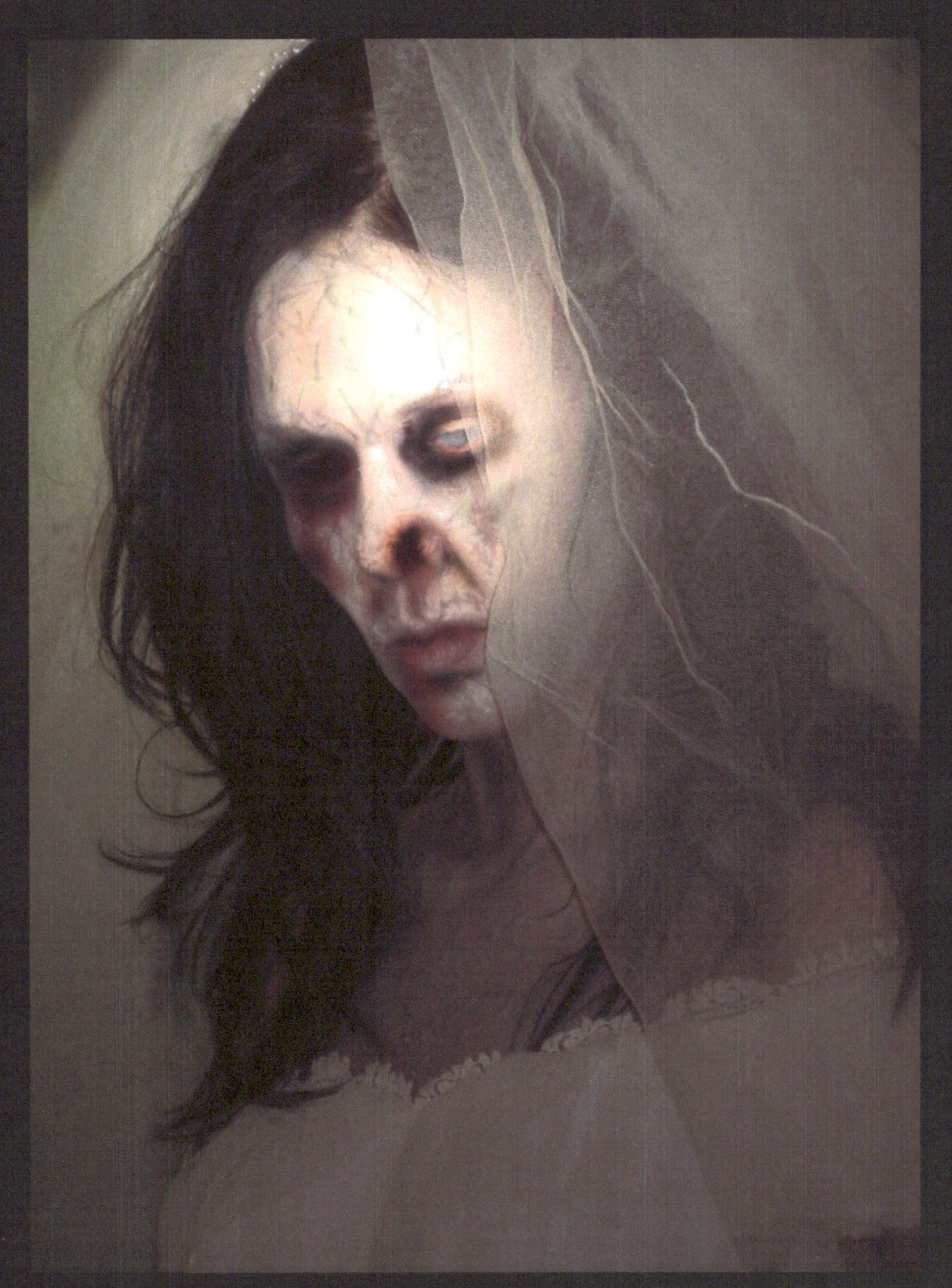

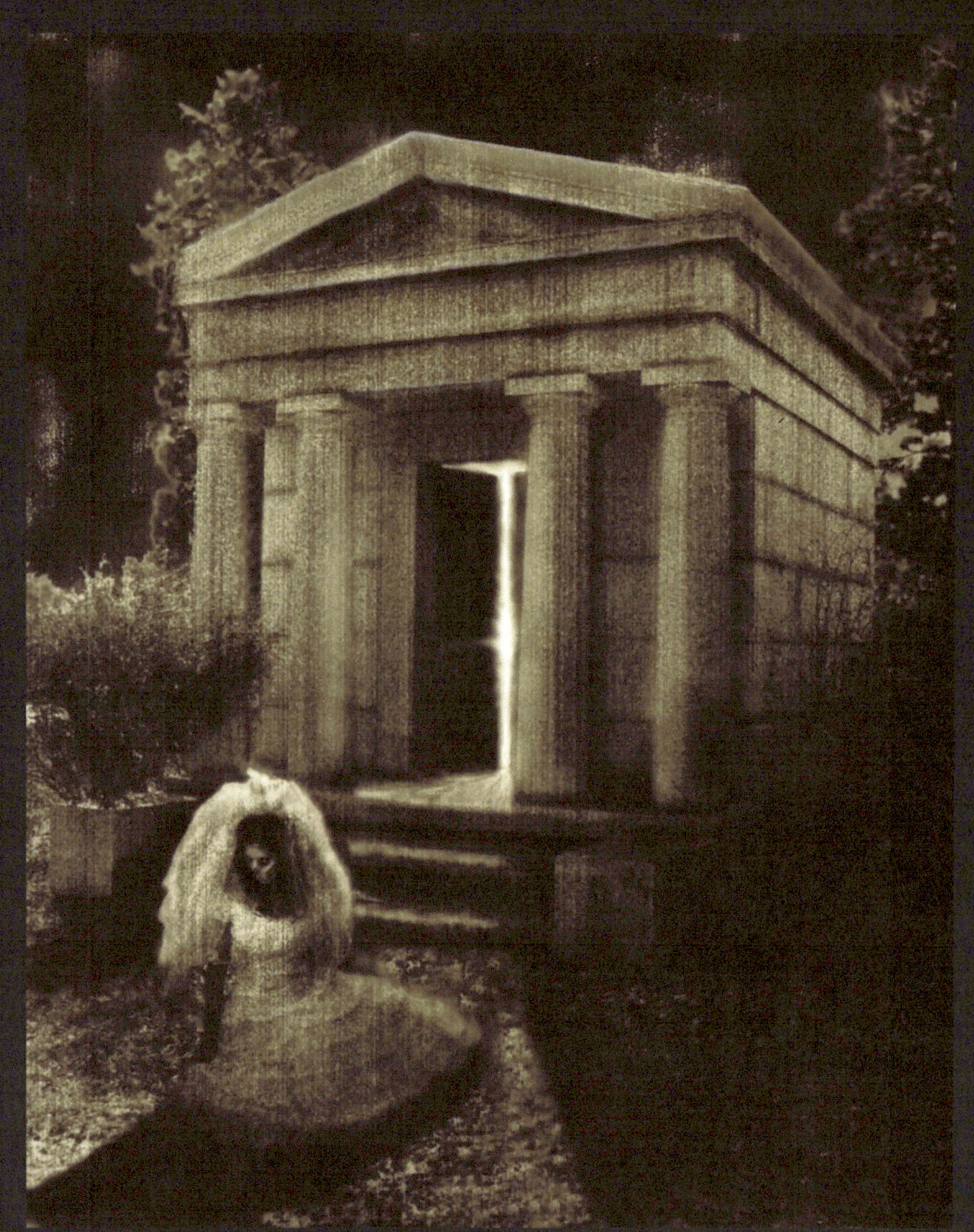

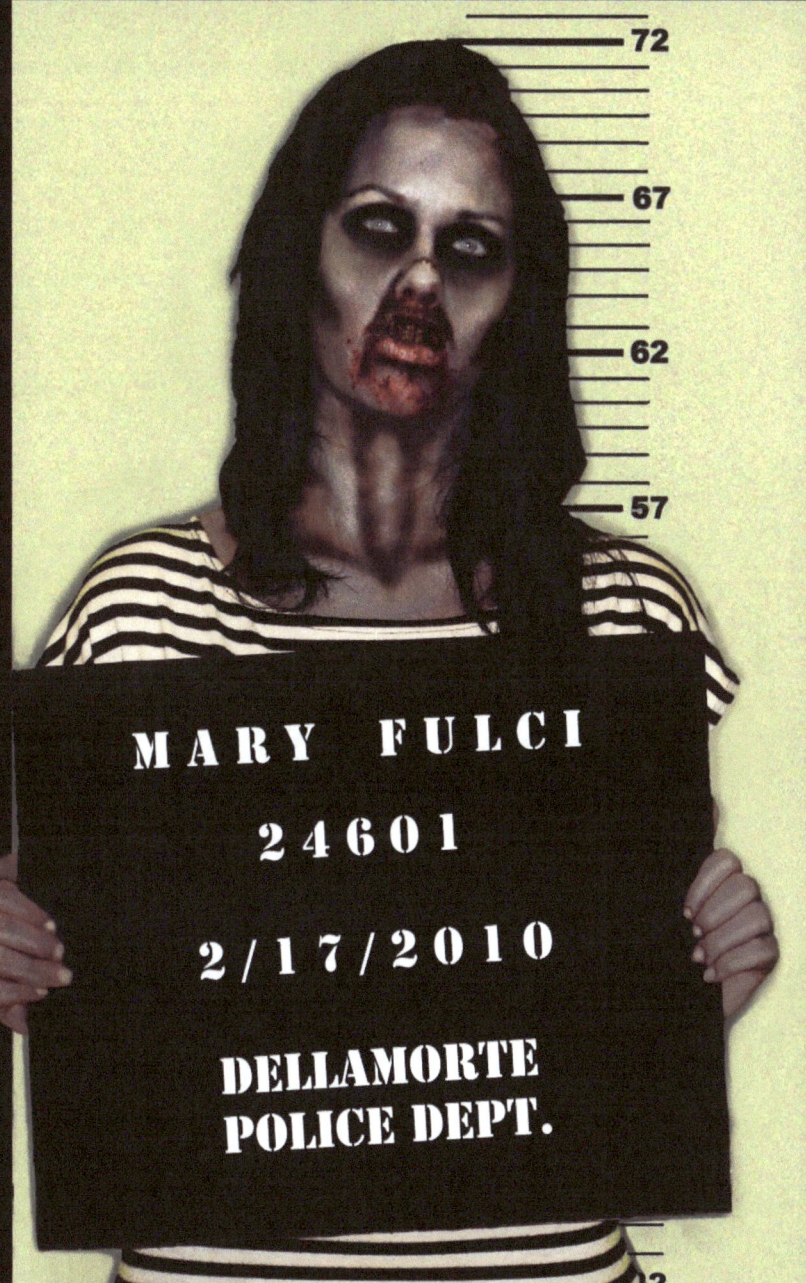

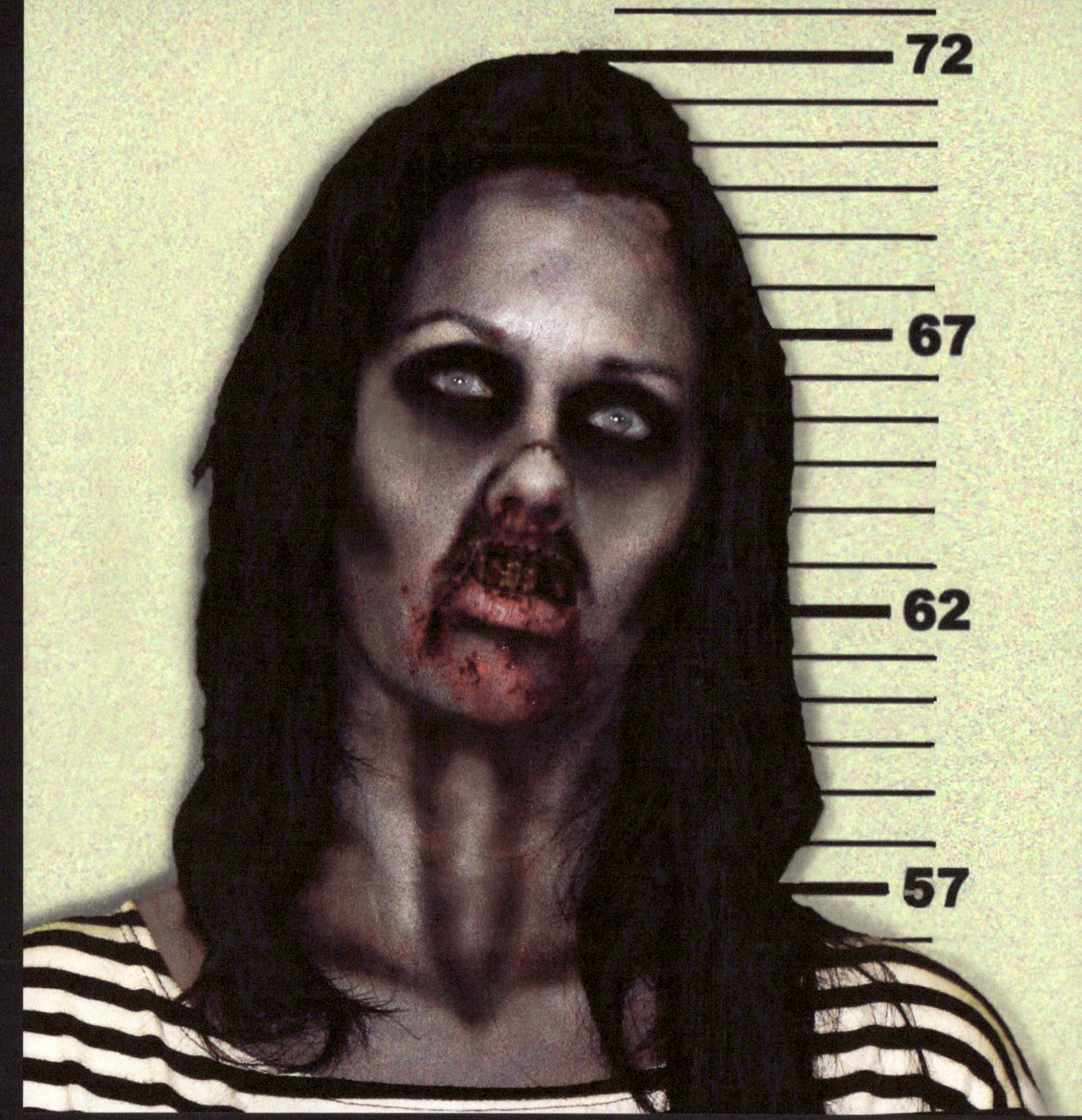

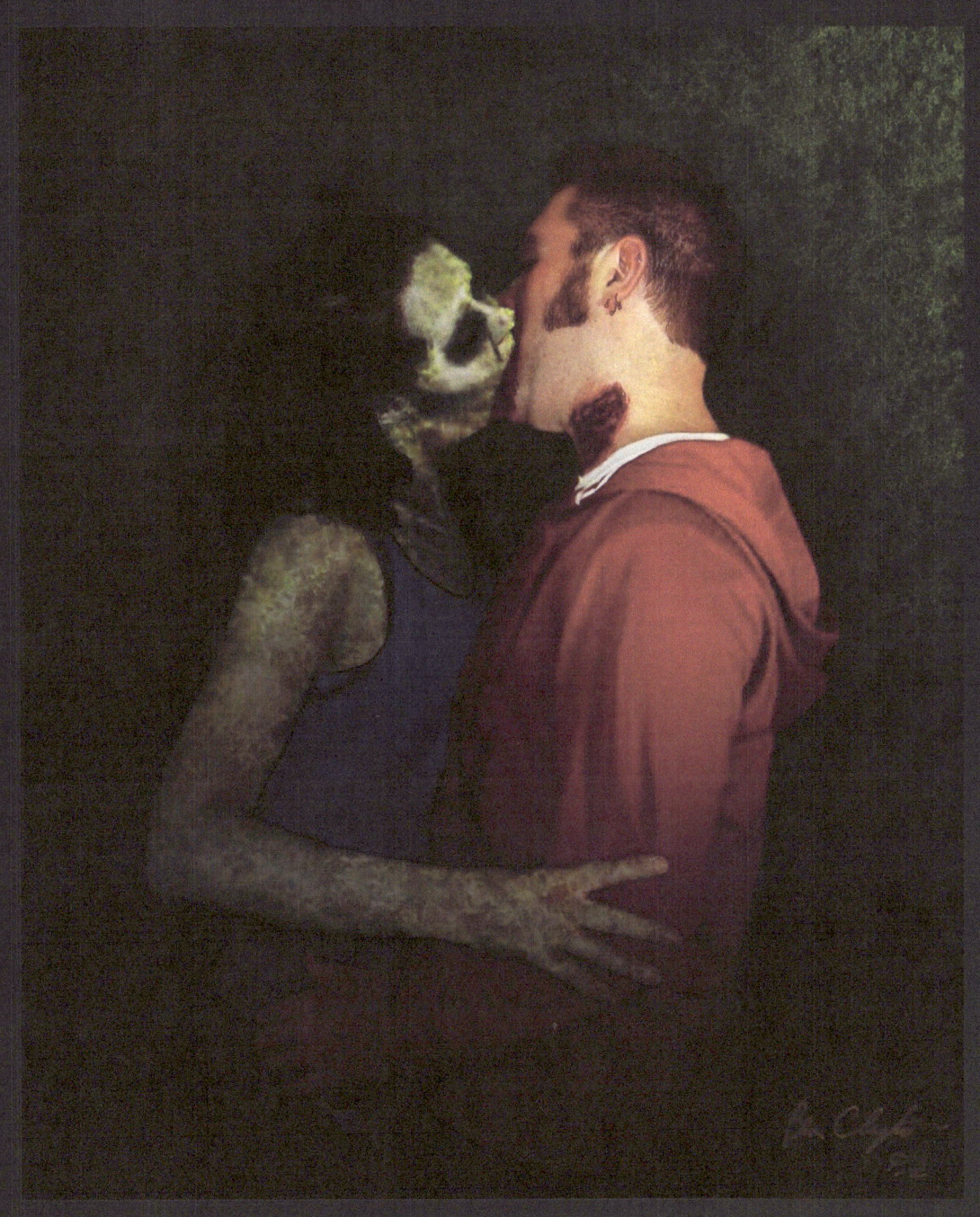

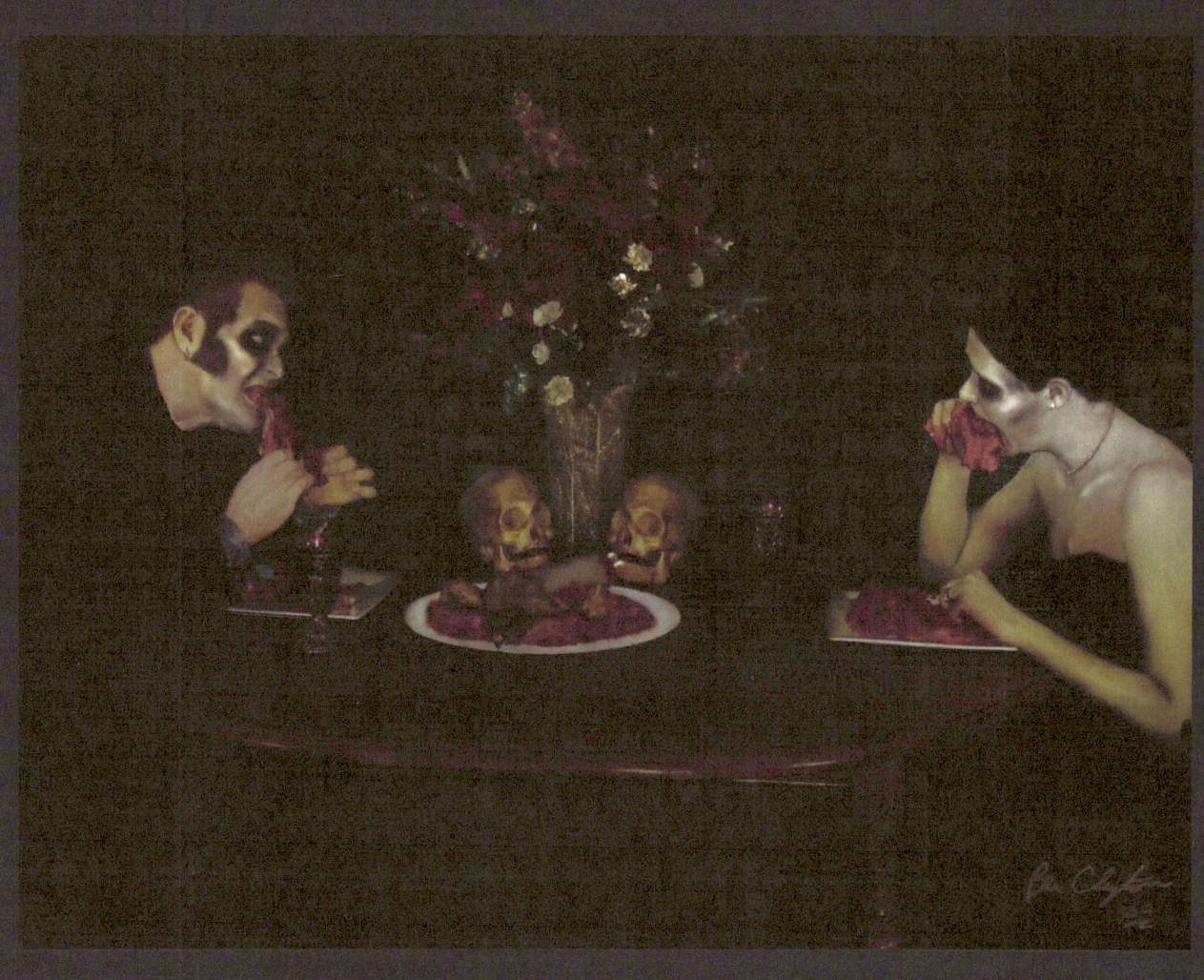

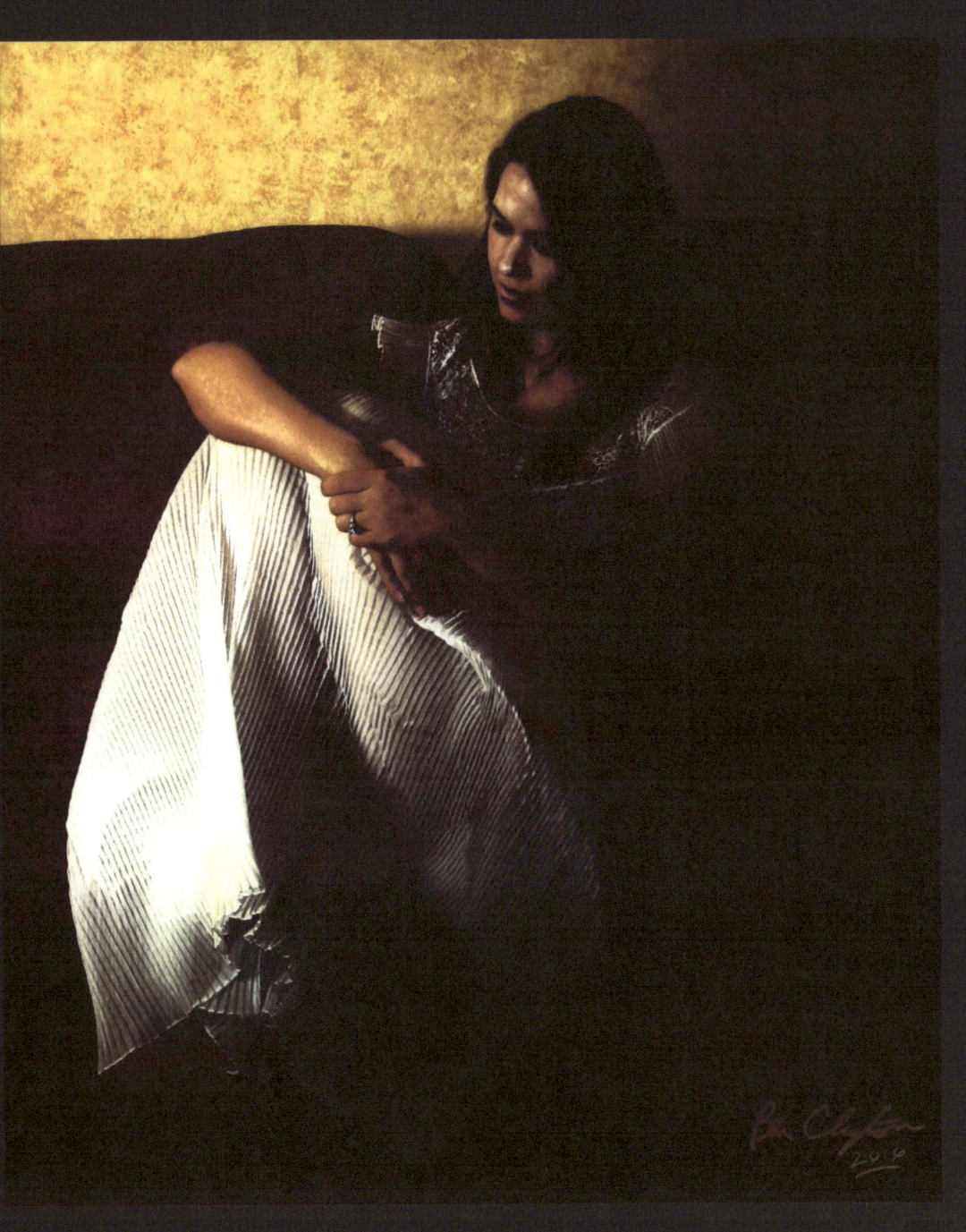

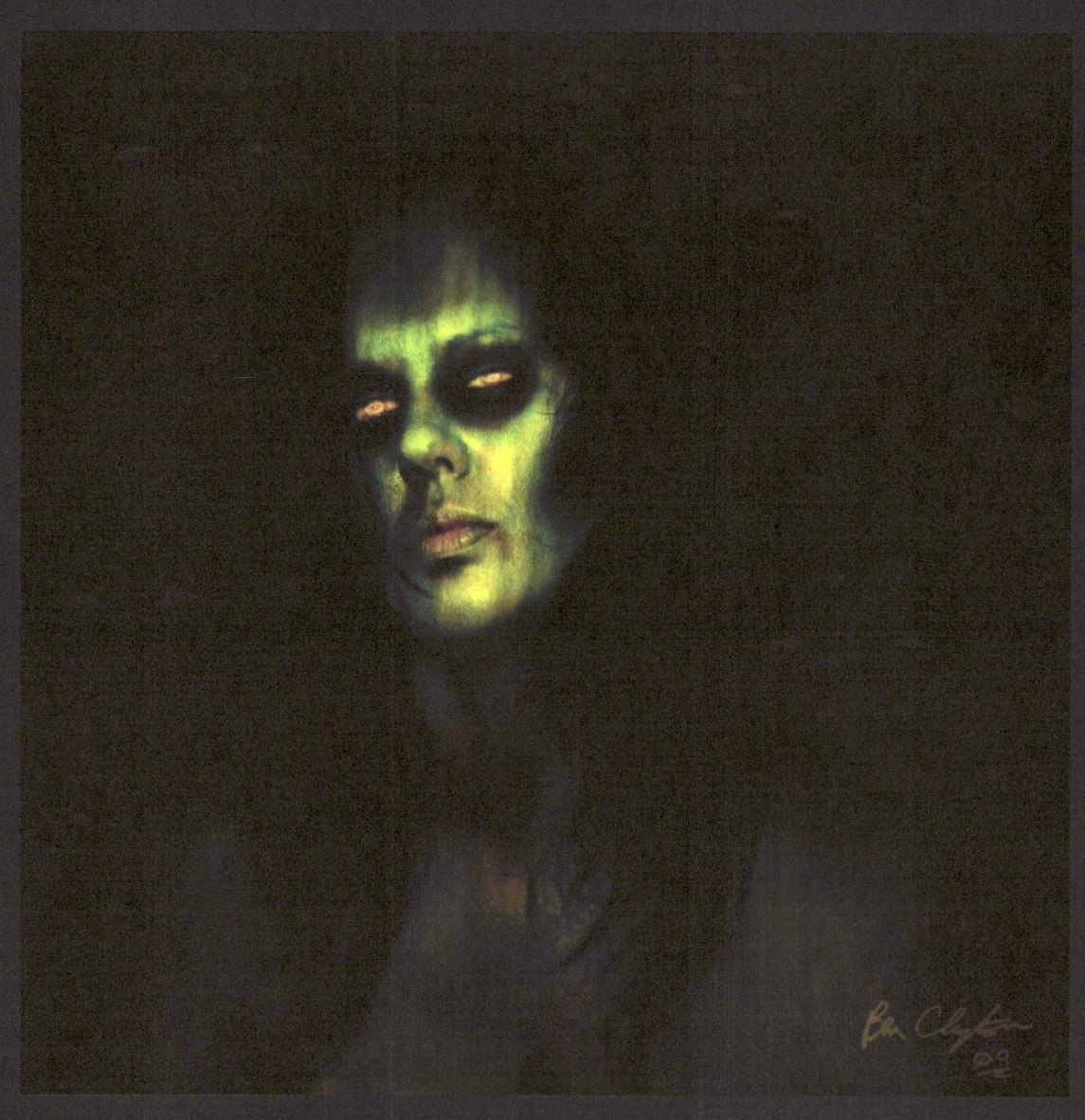

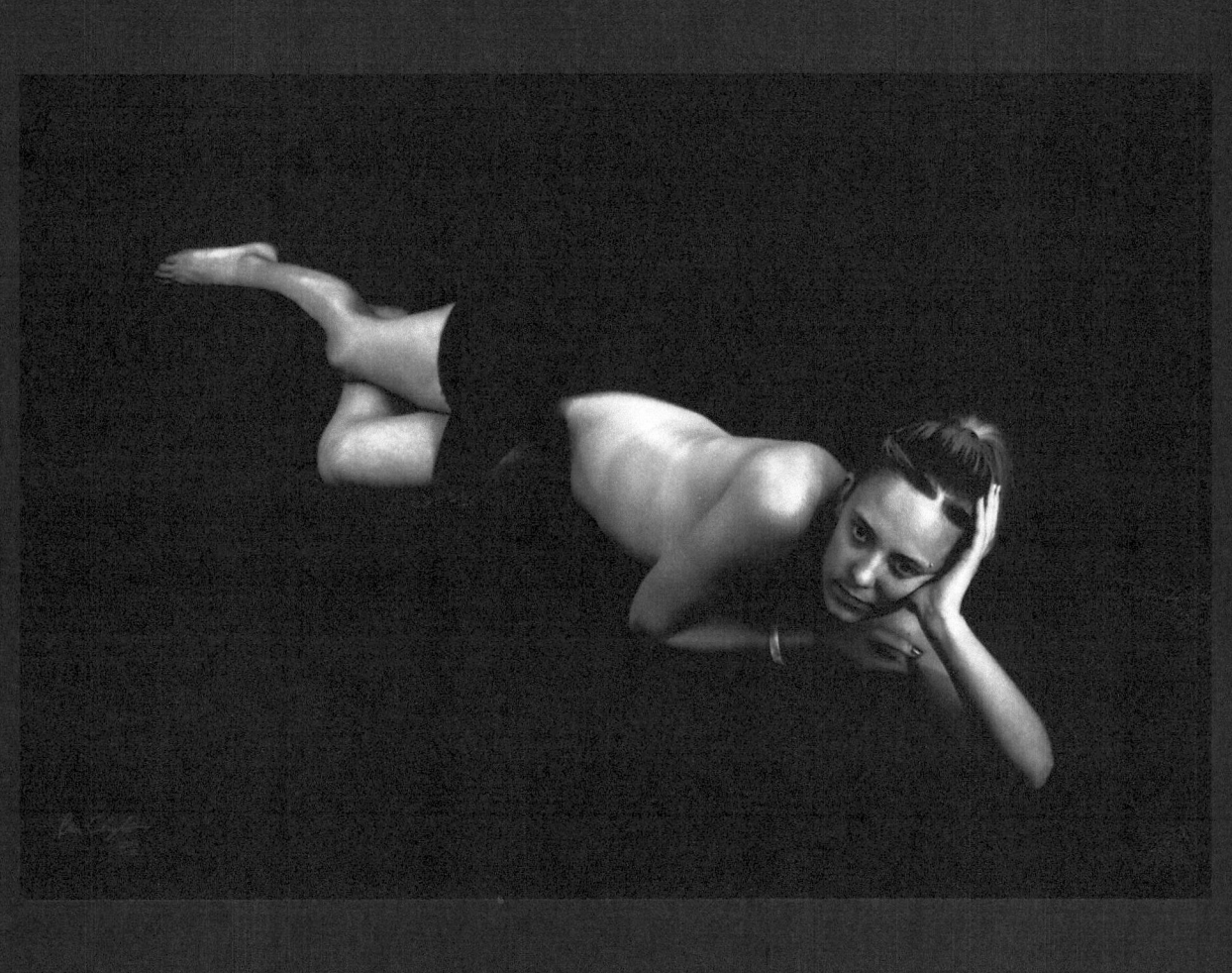

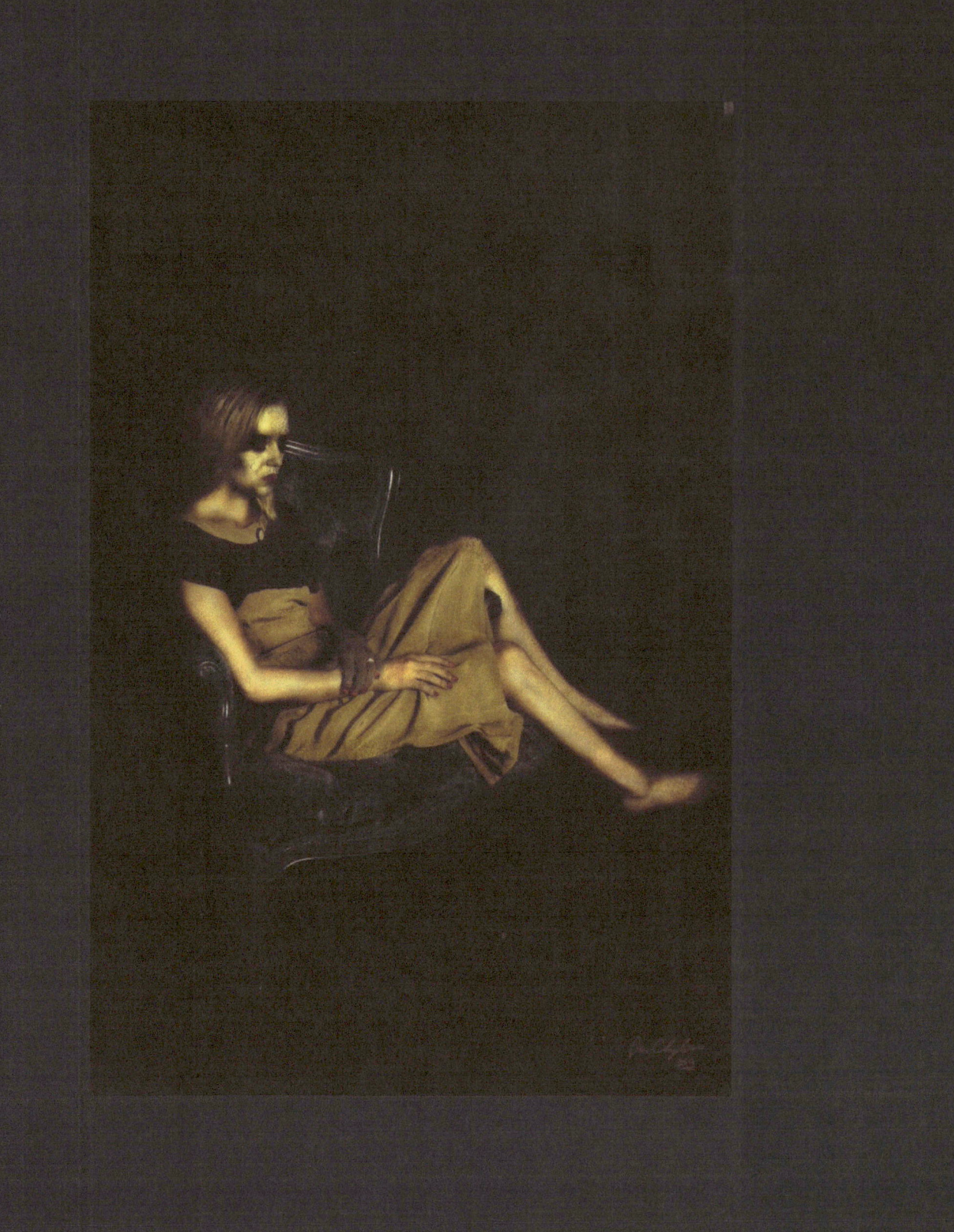

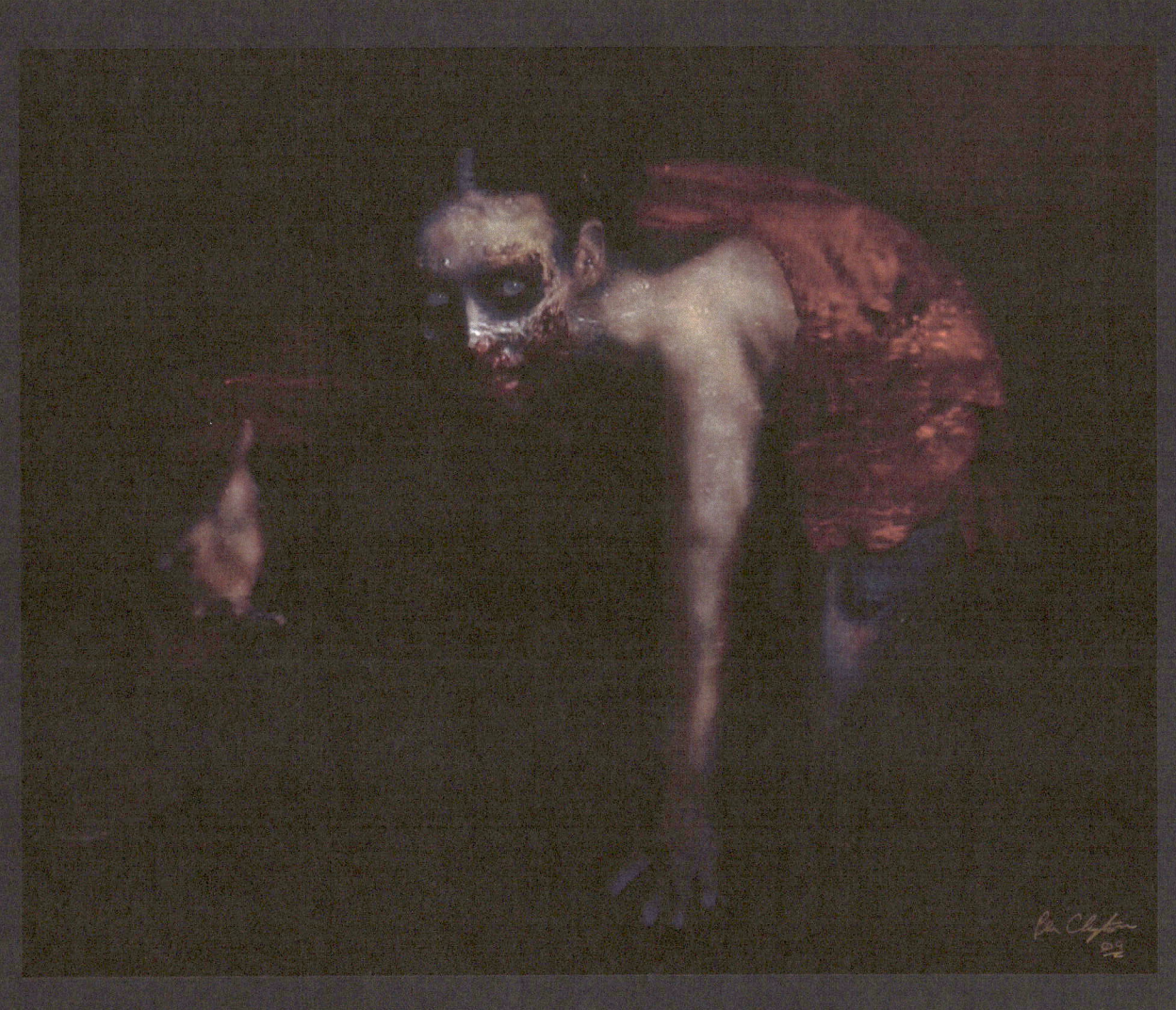

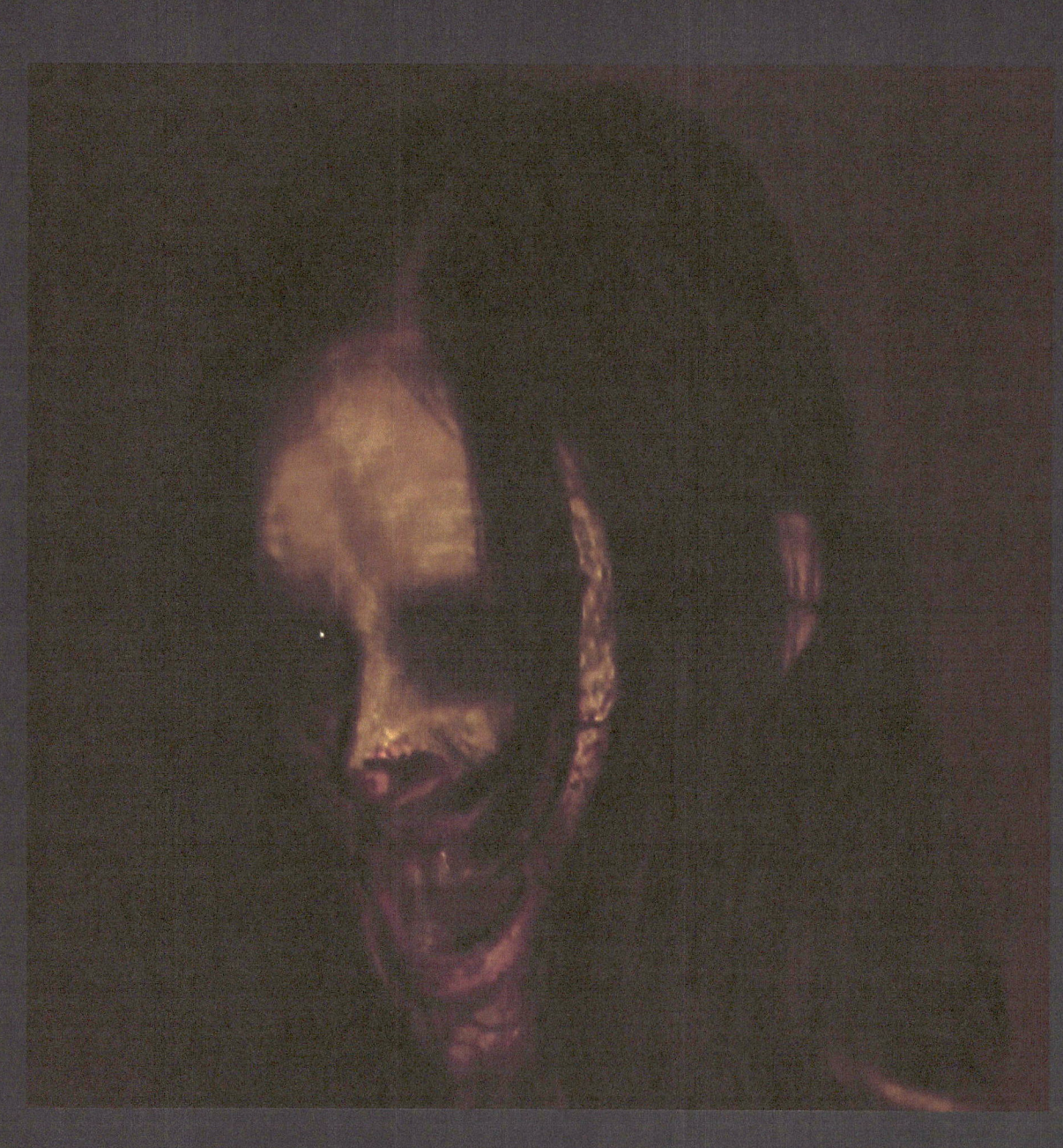

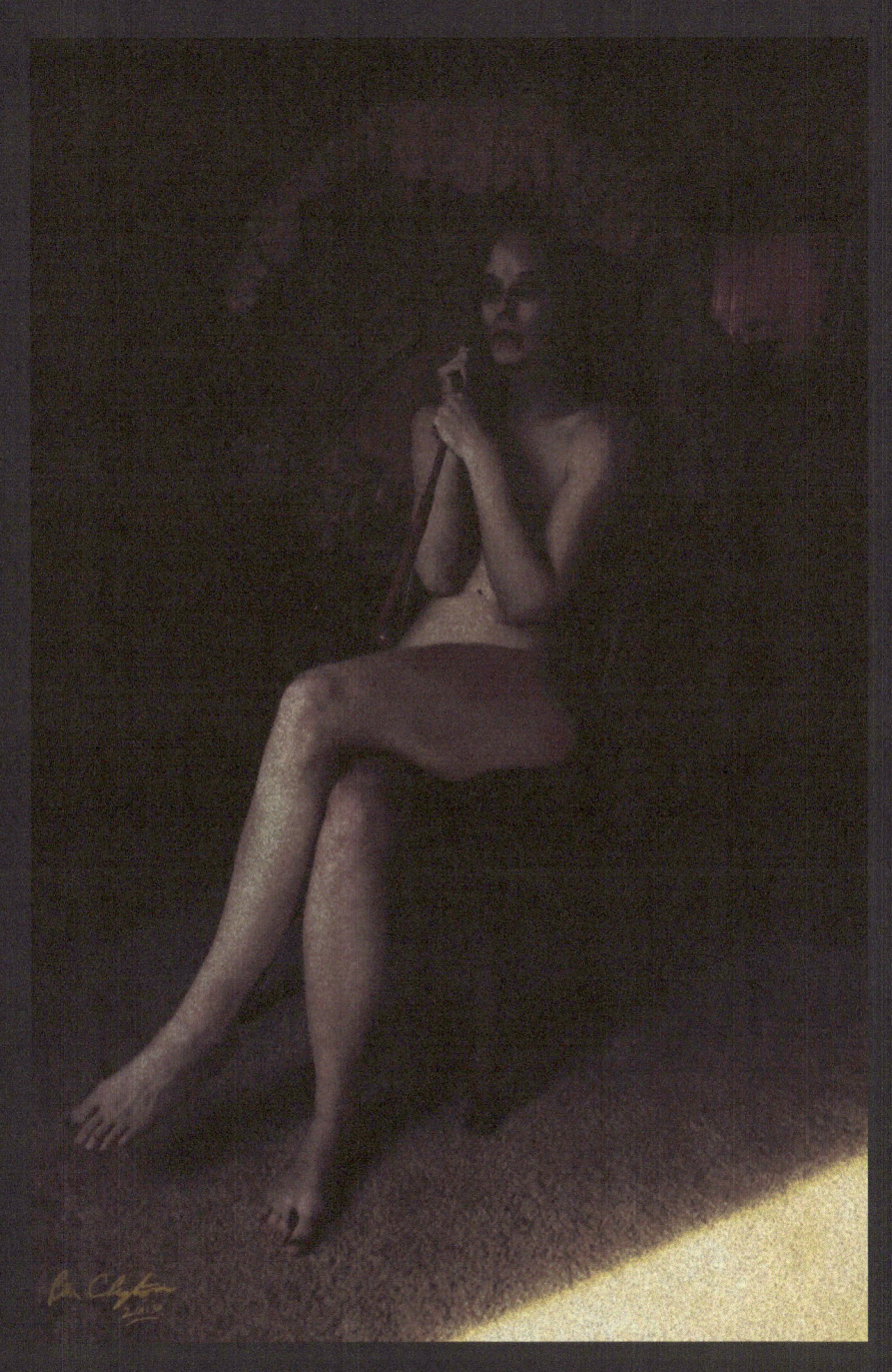

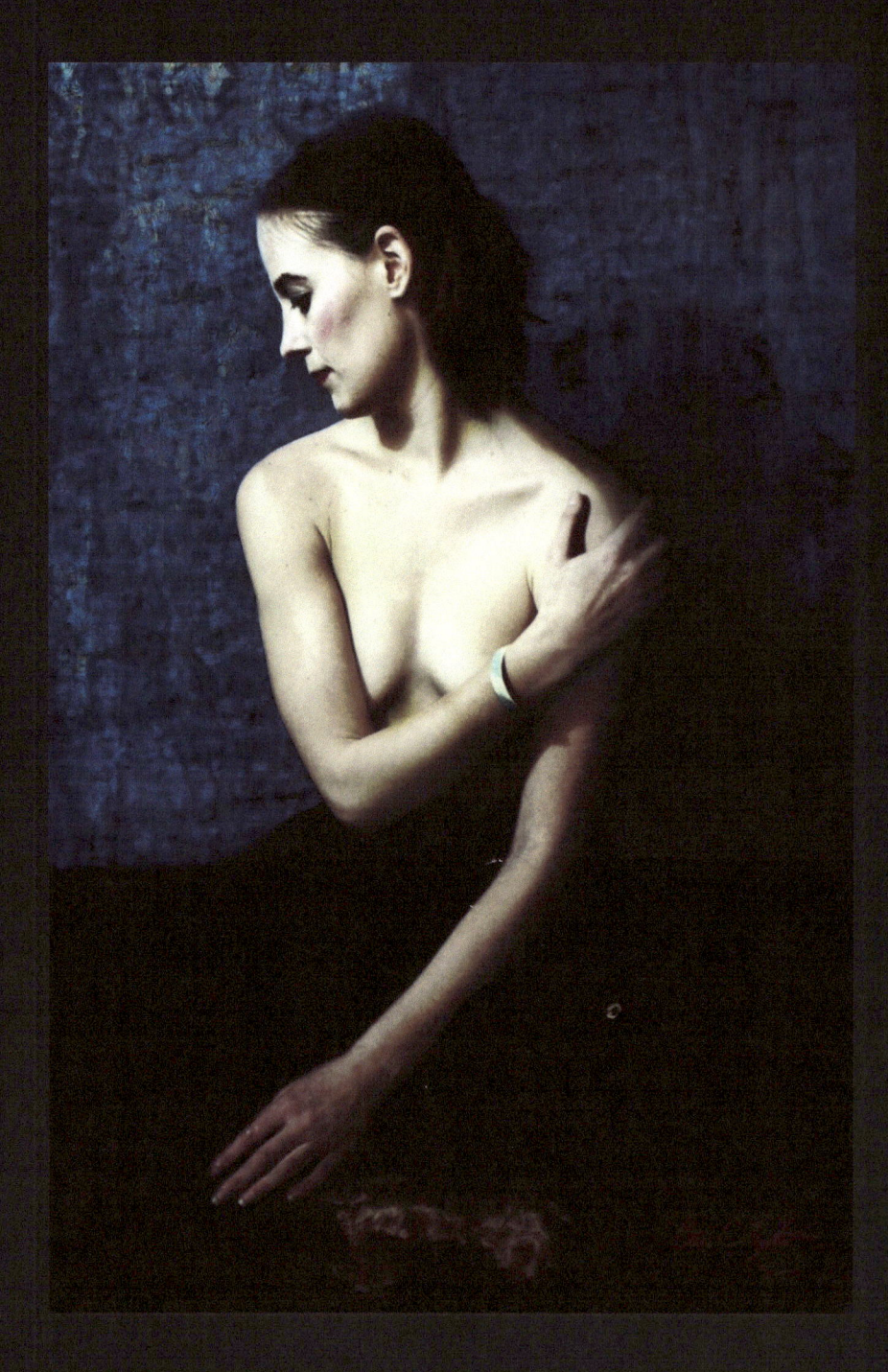

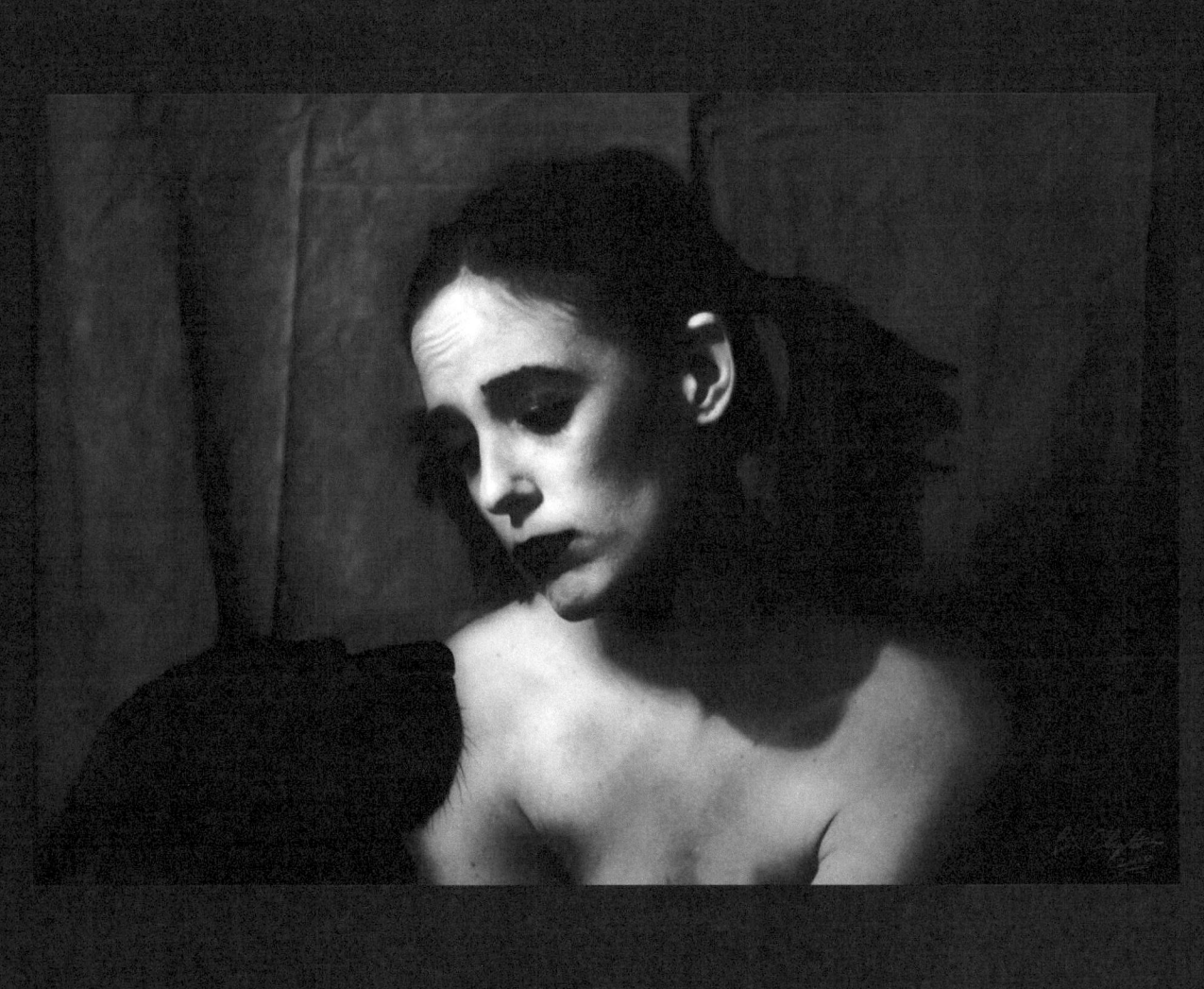

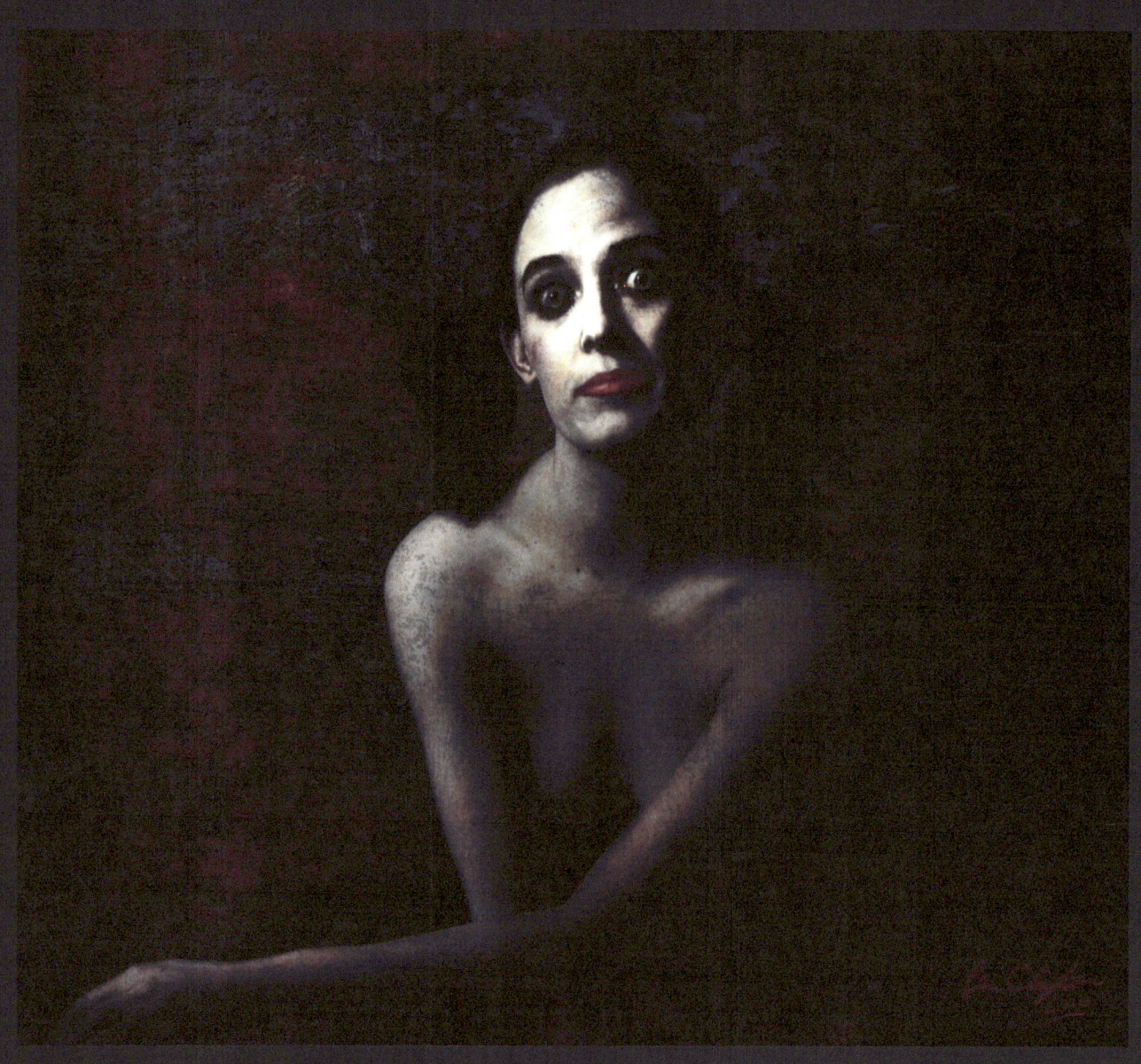

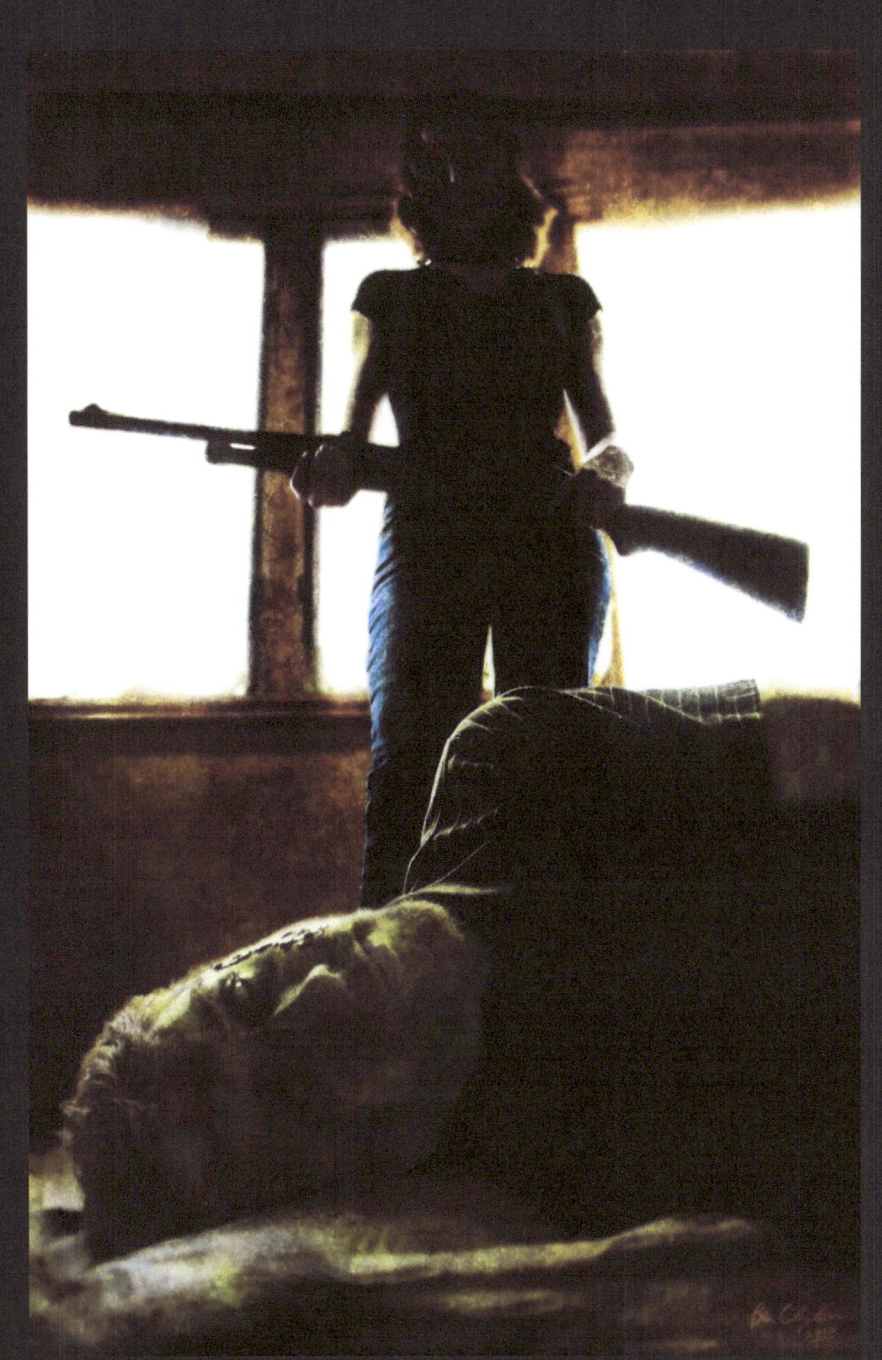

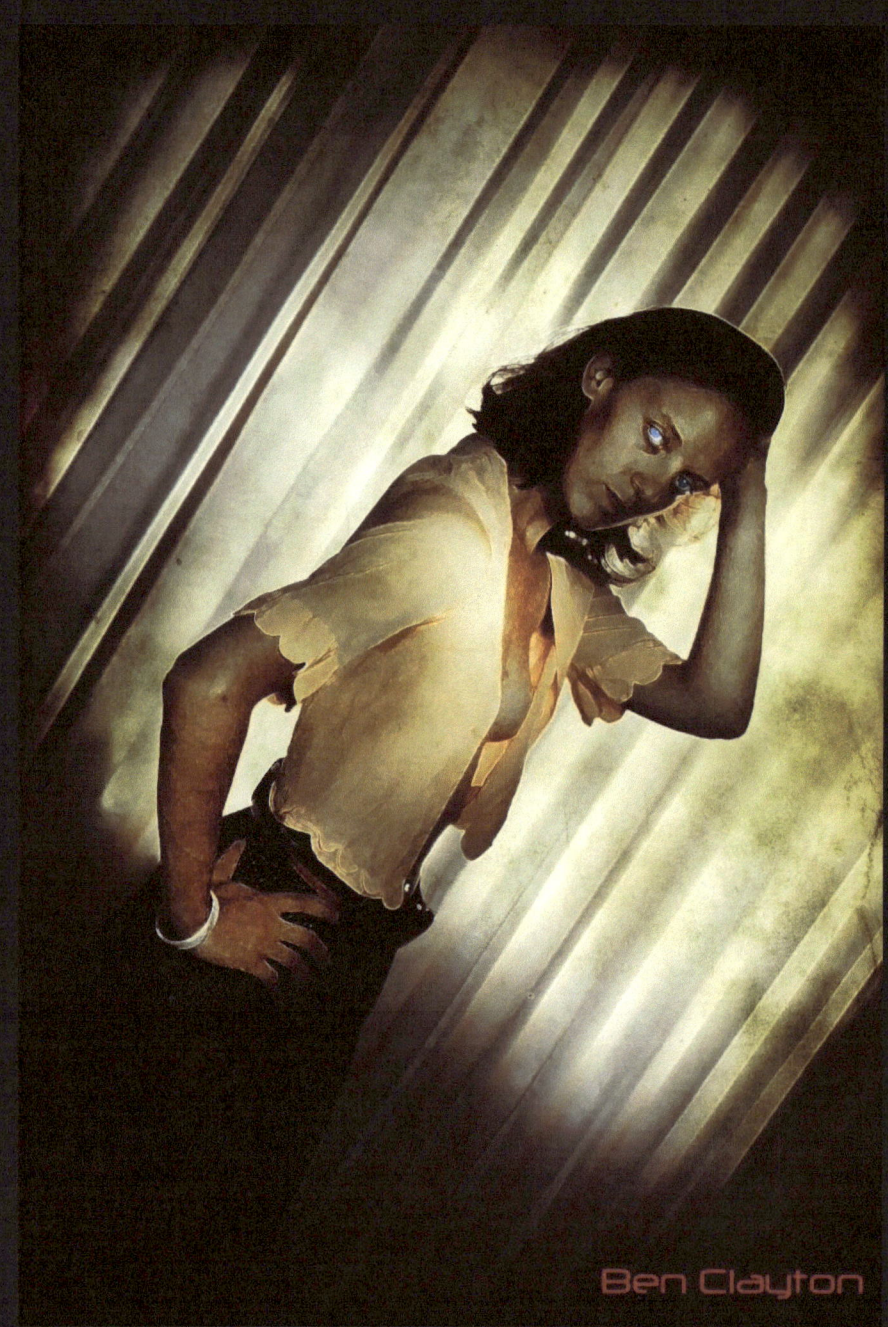

Ben Clayton

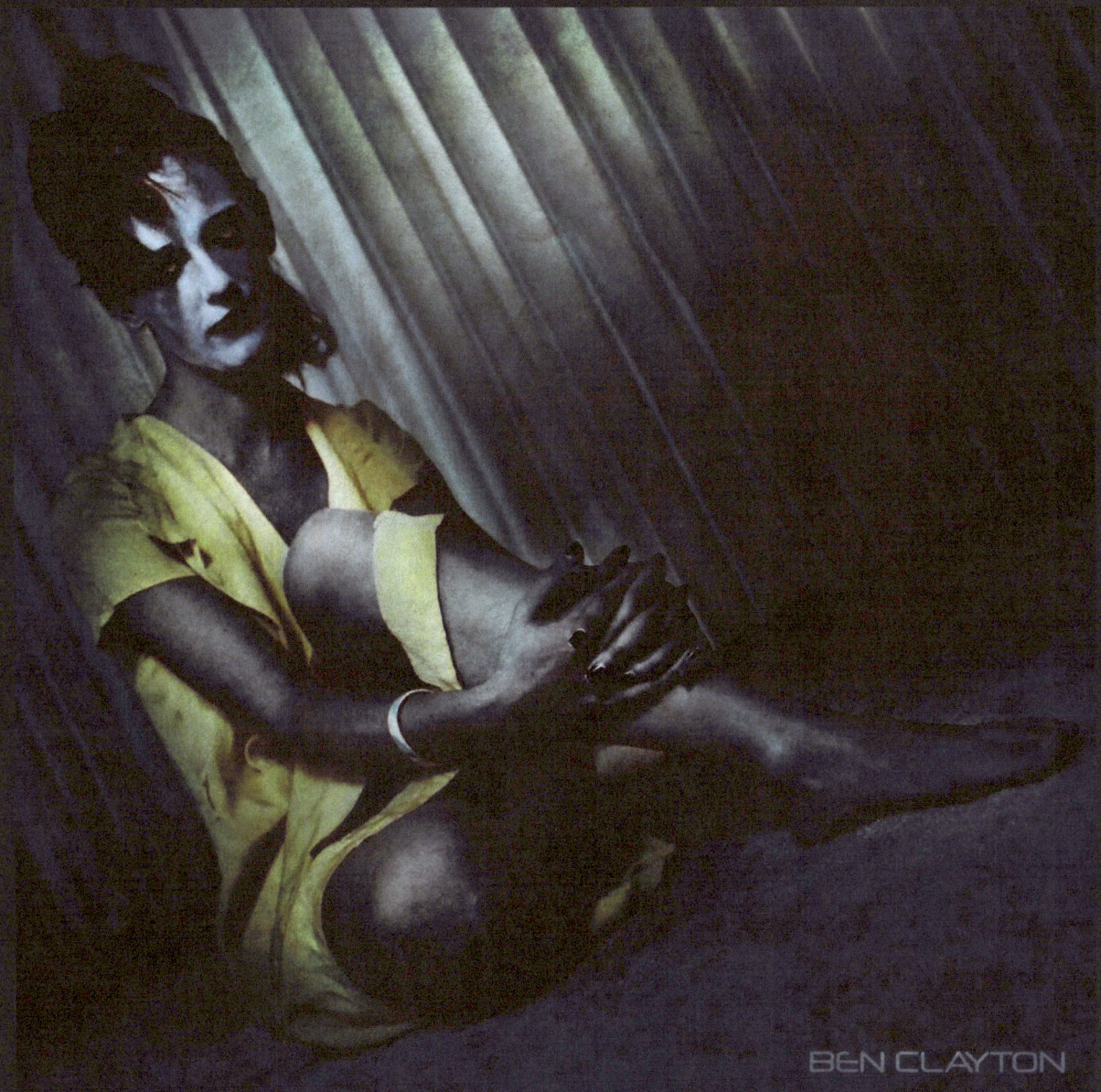
BEN CLAYTON

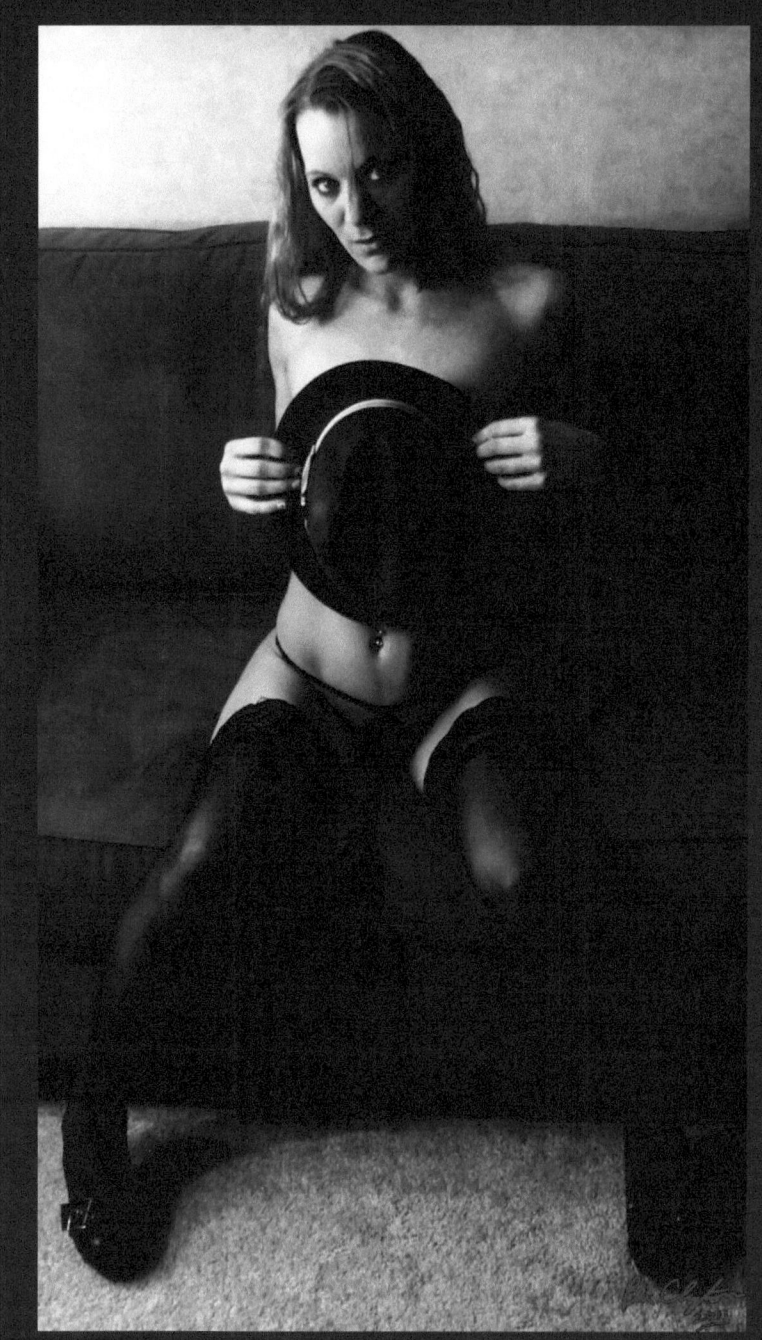

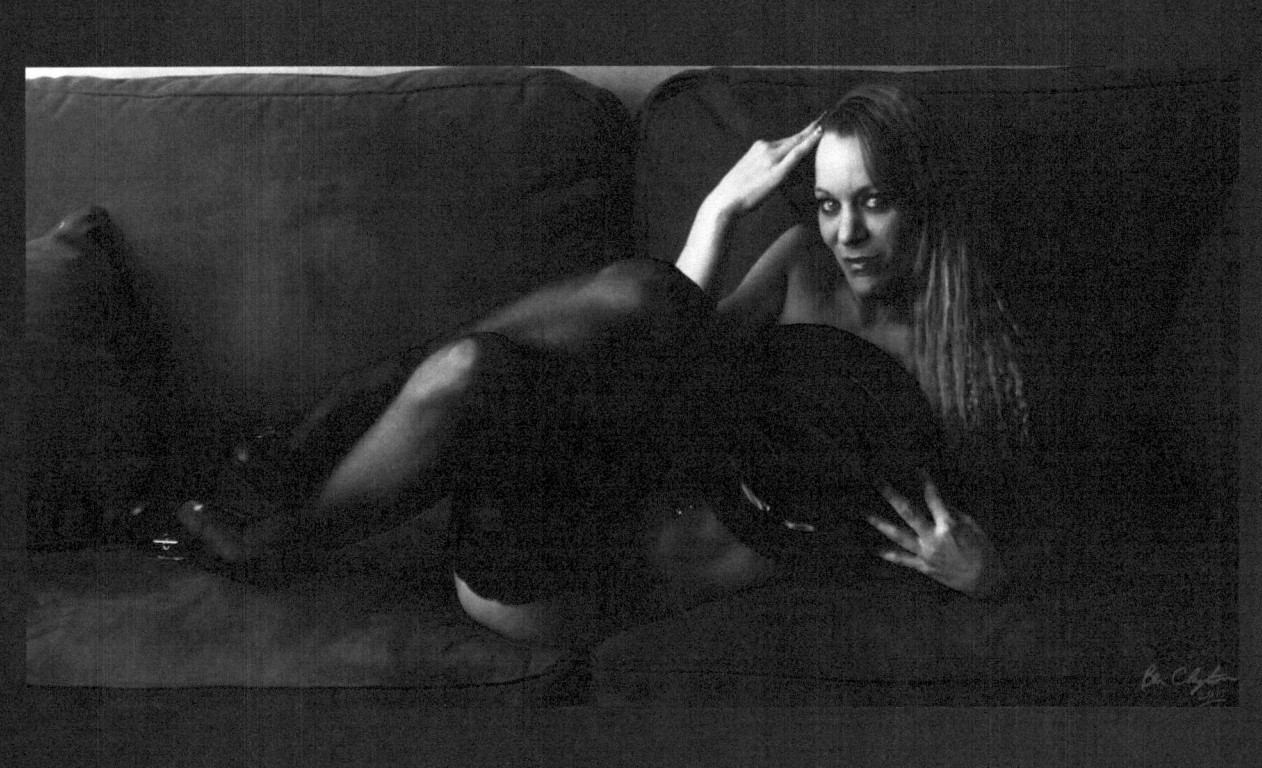

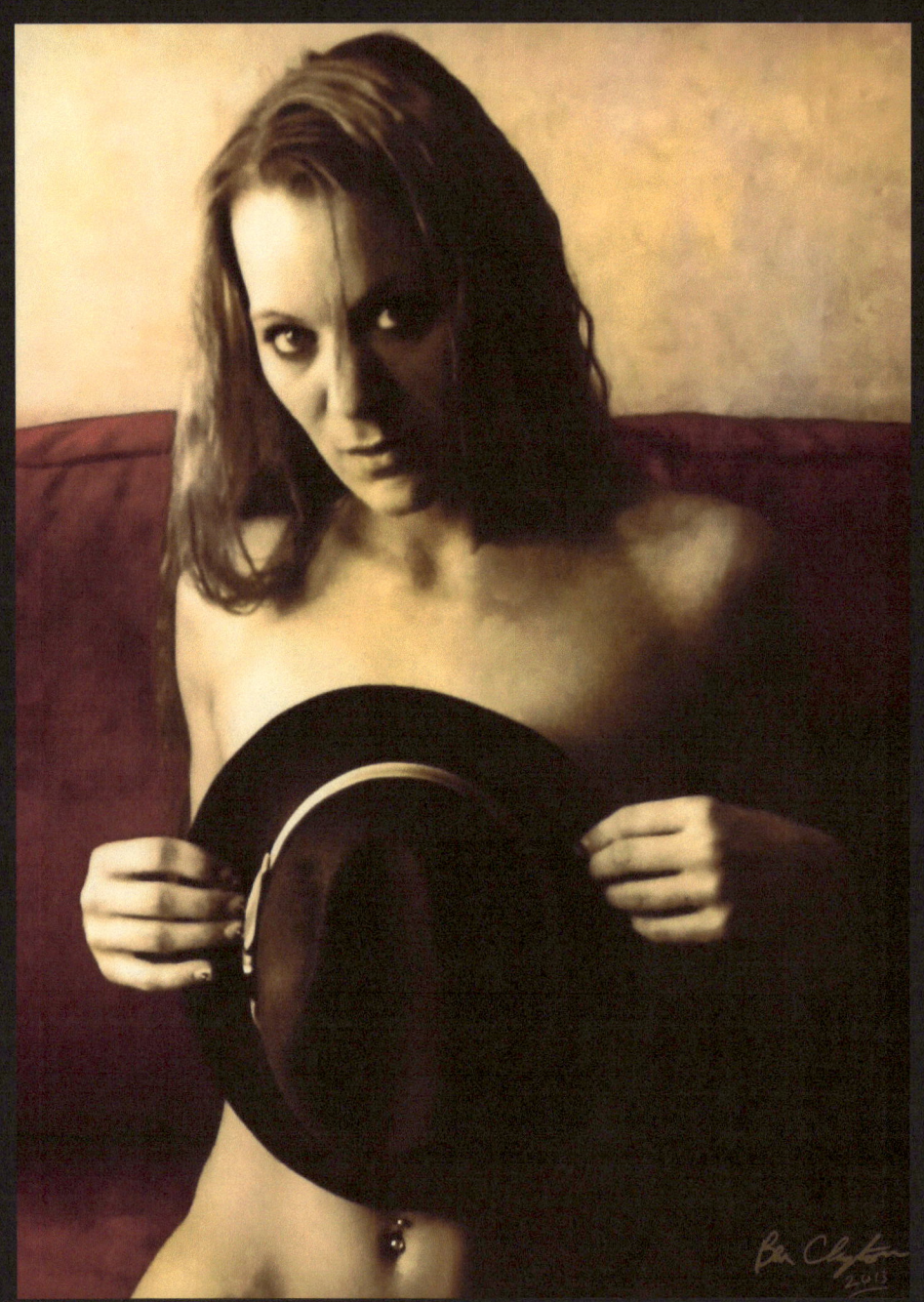

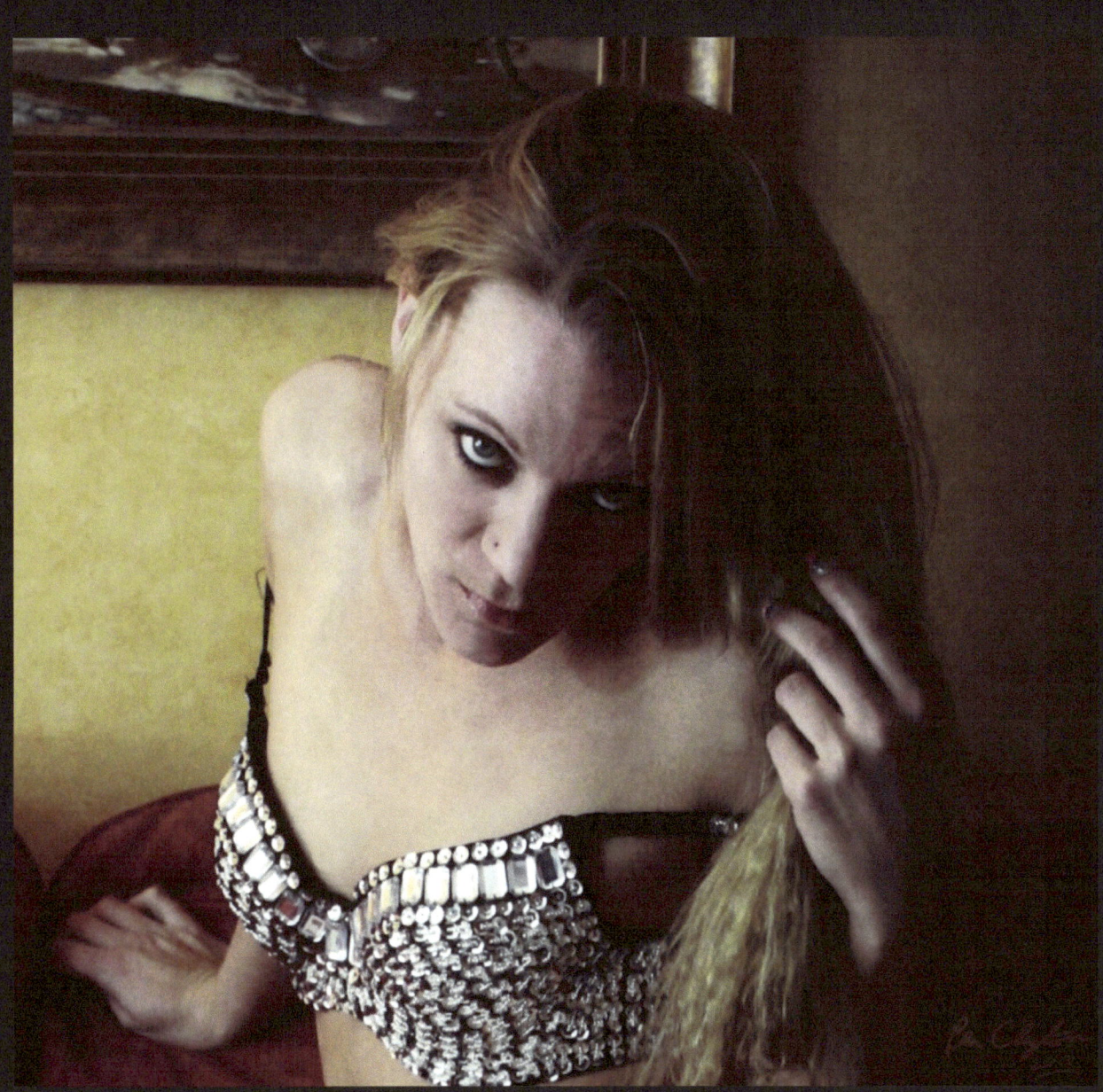

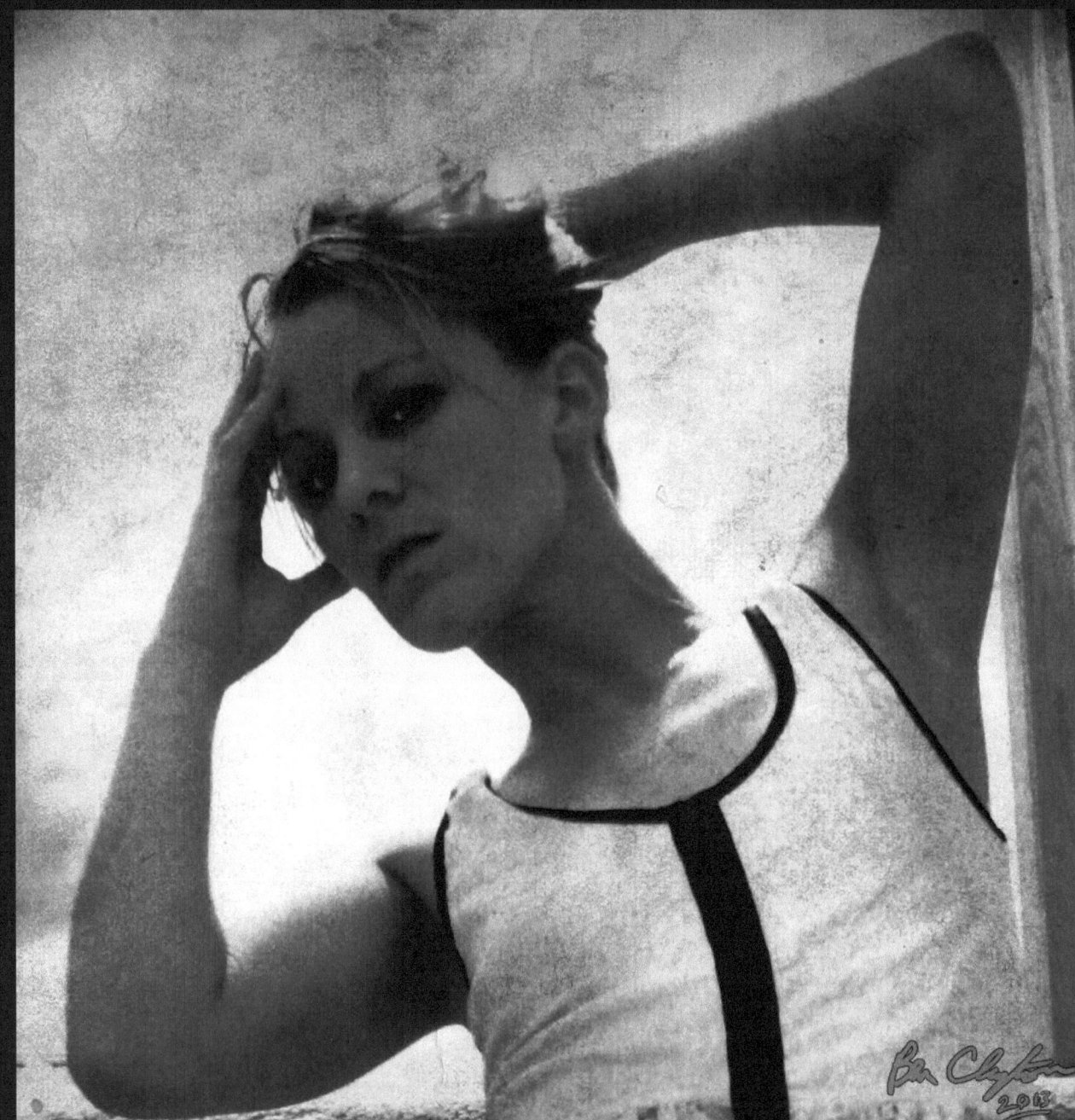

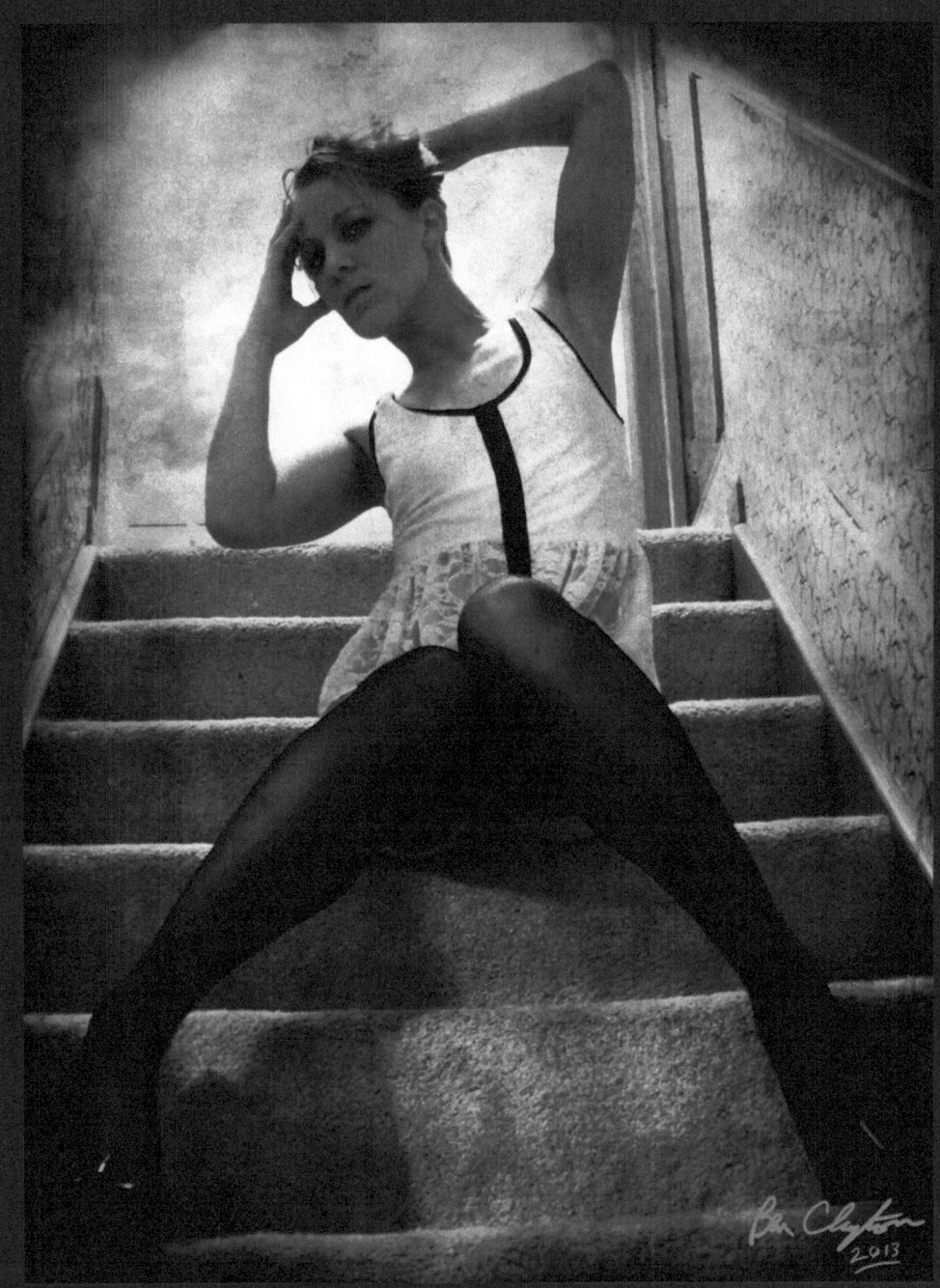

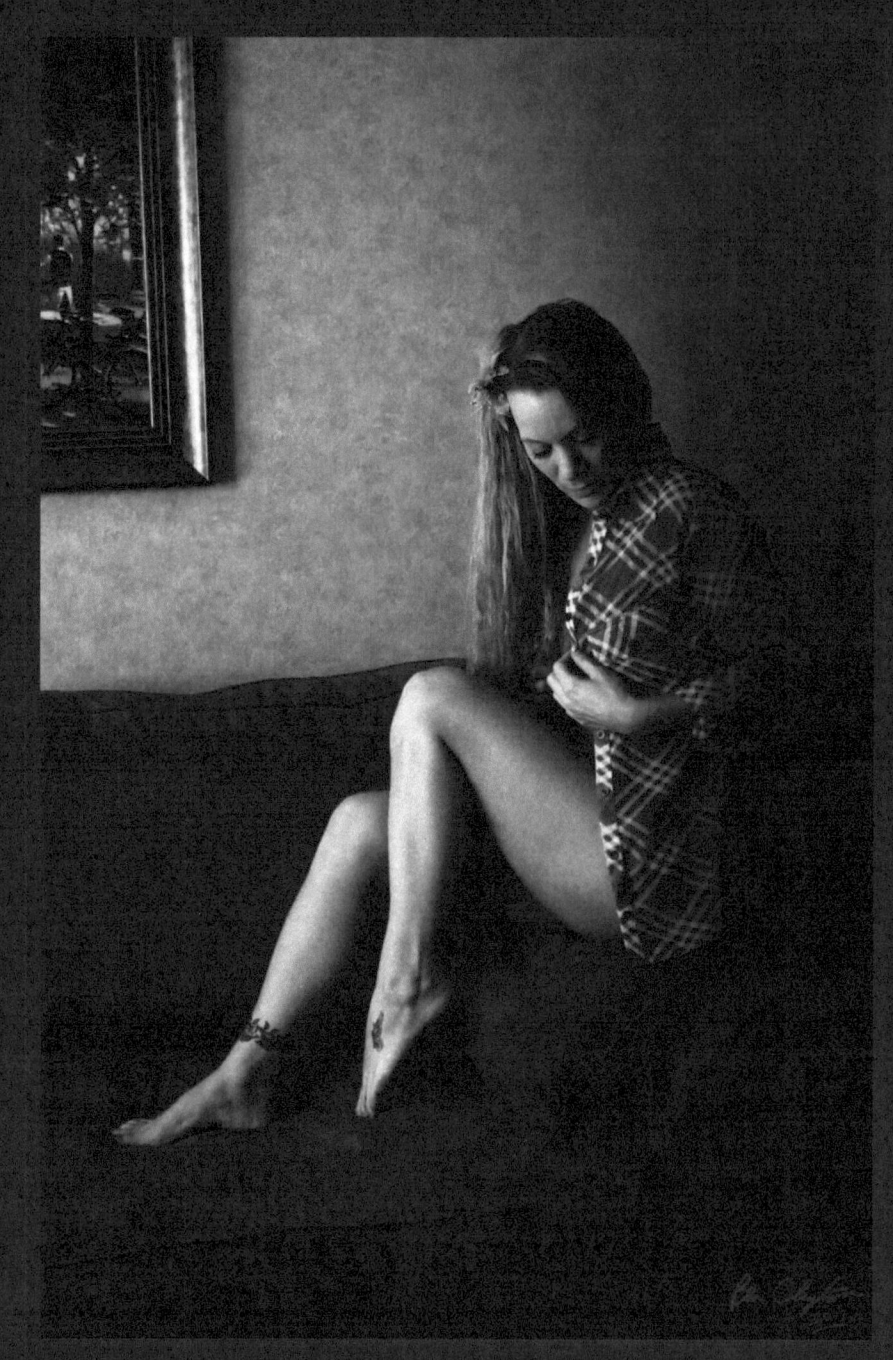

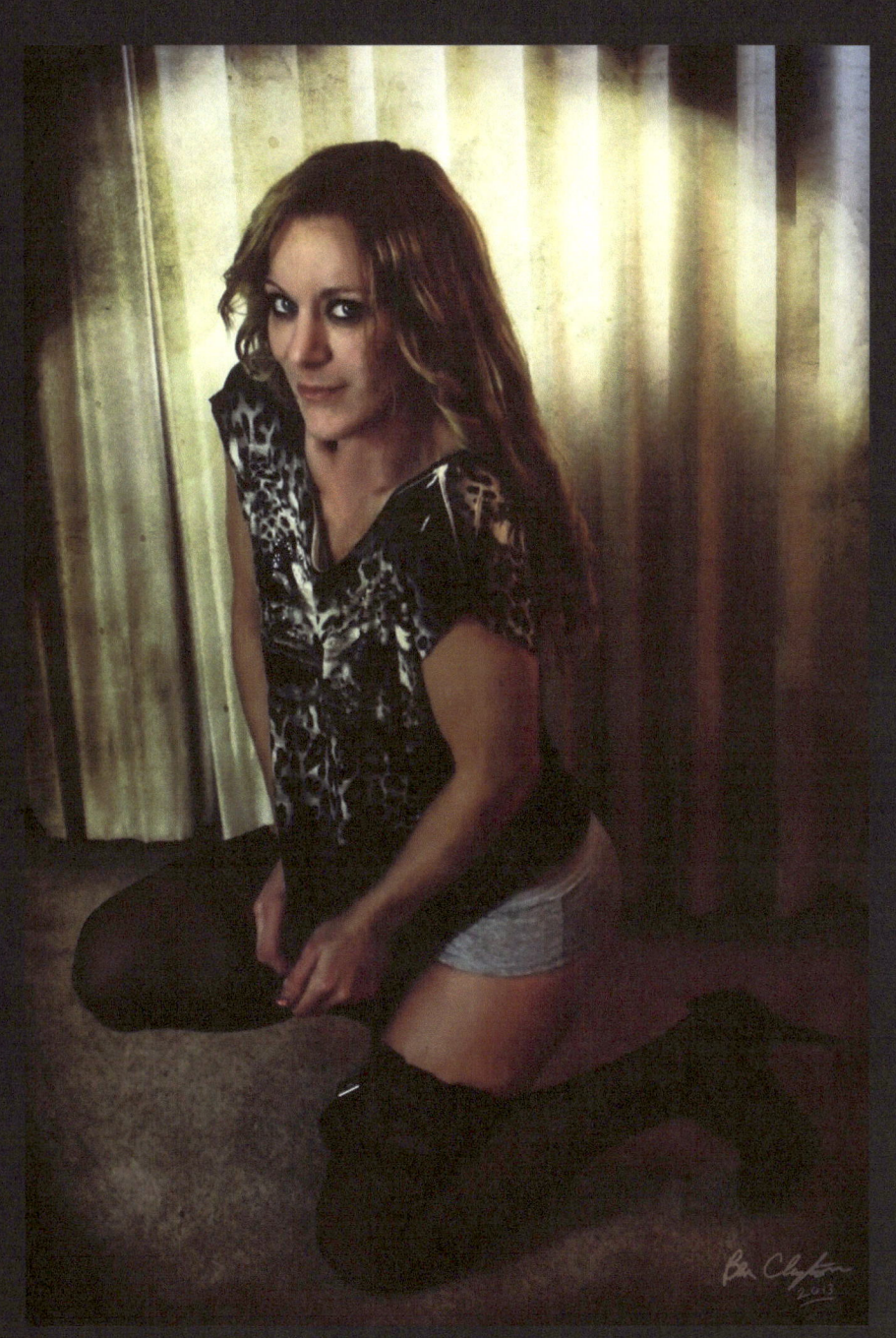

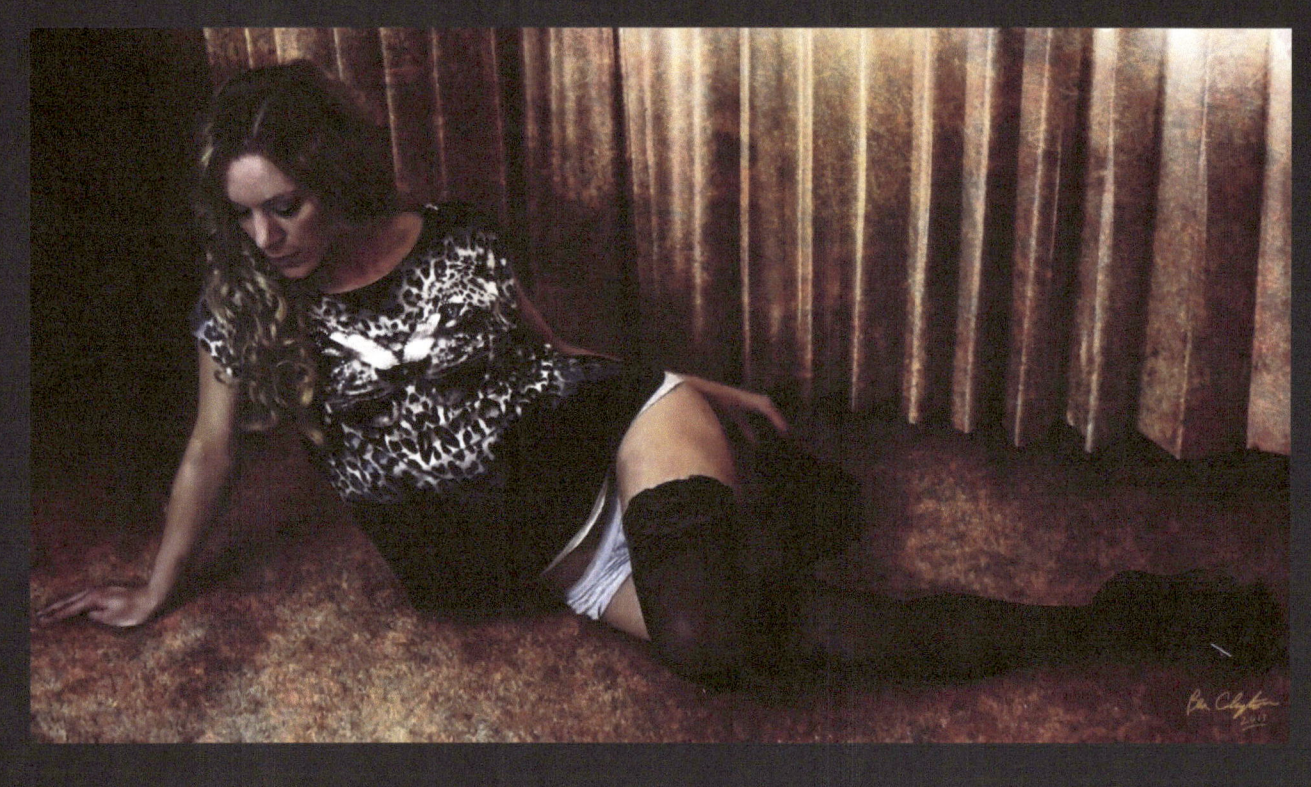

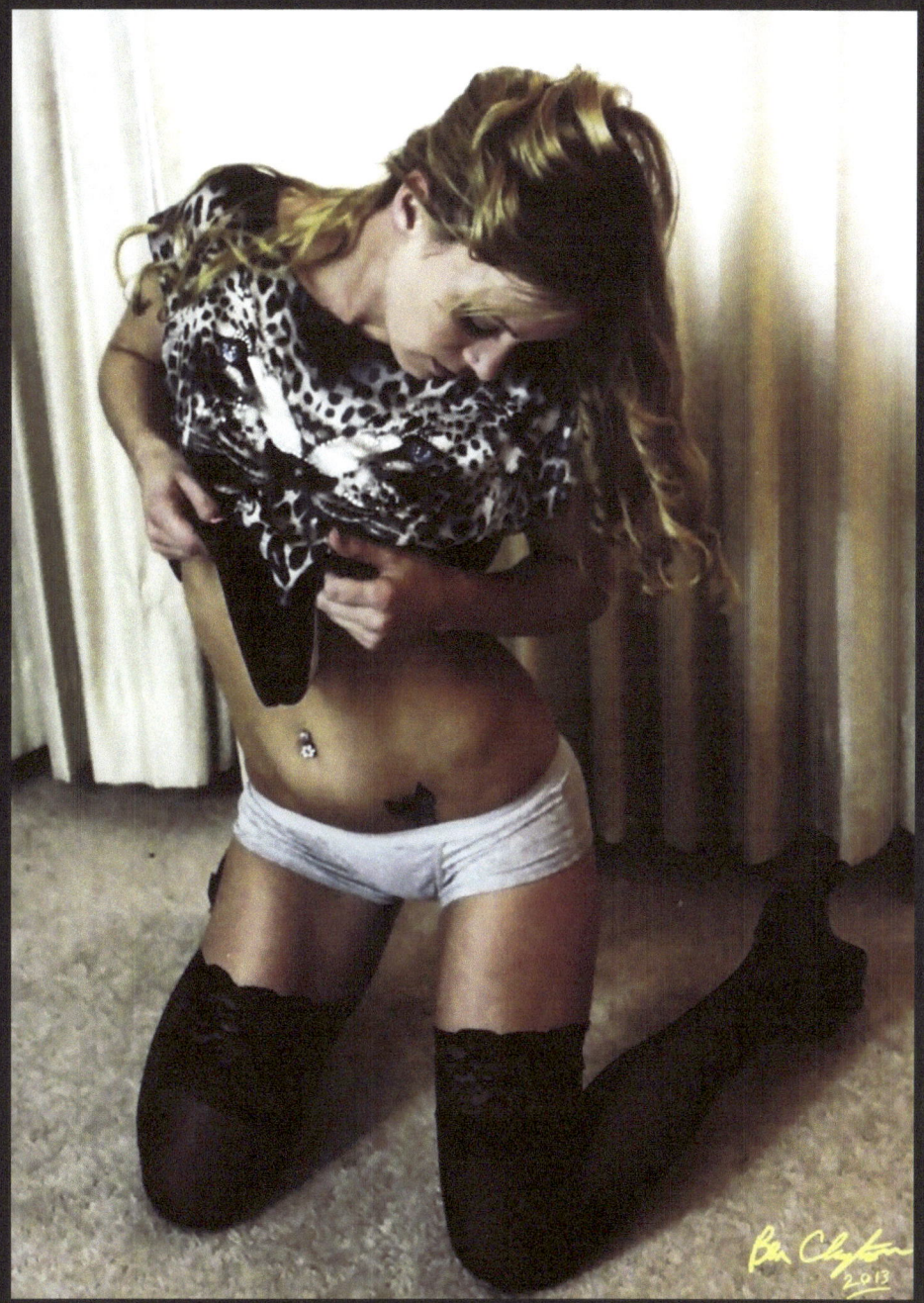

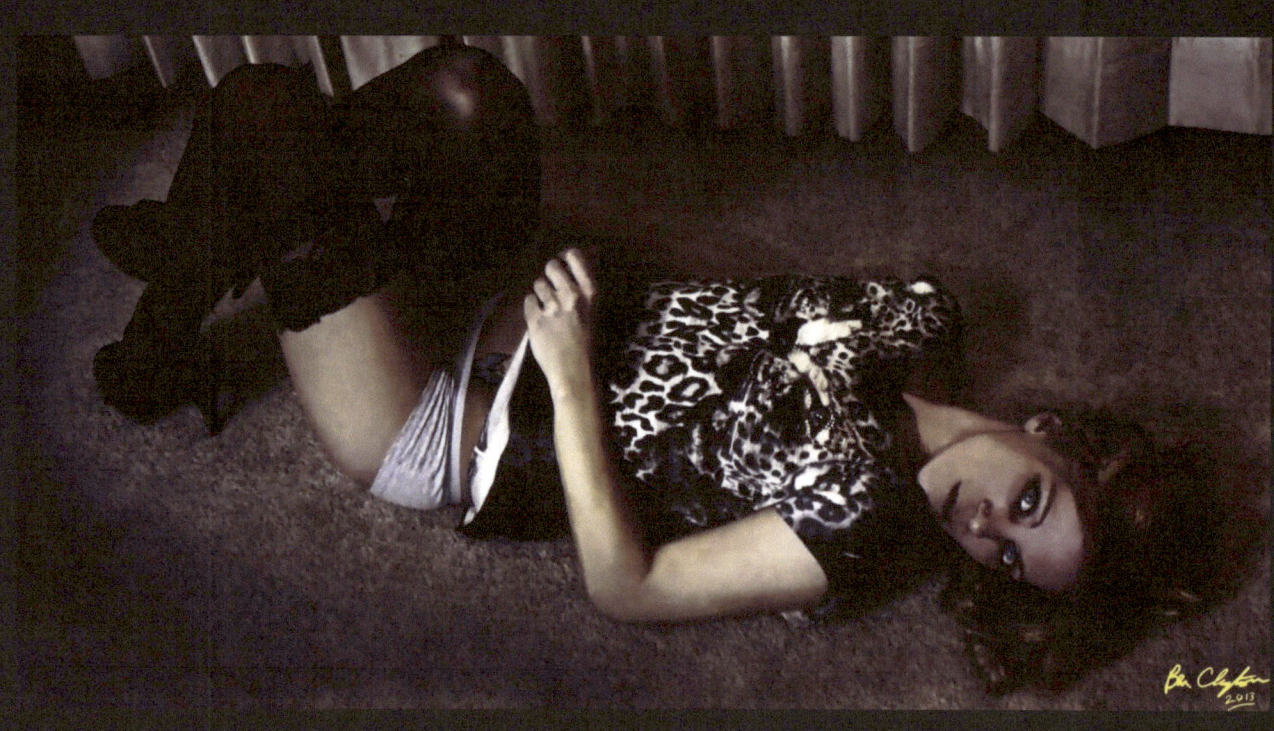

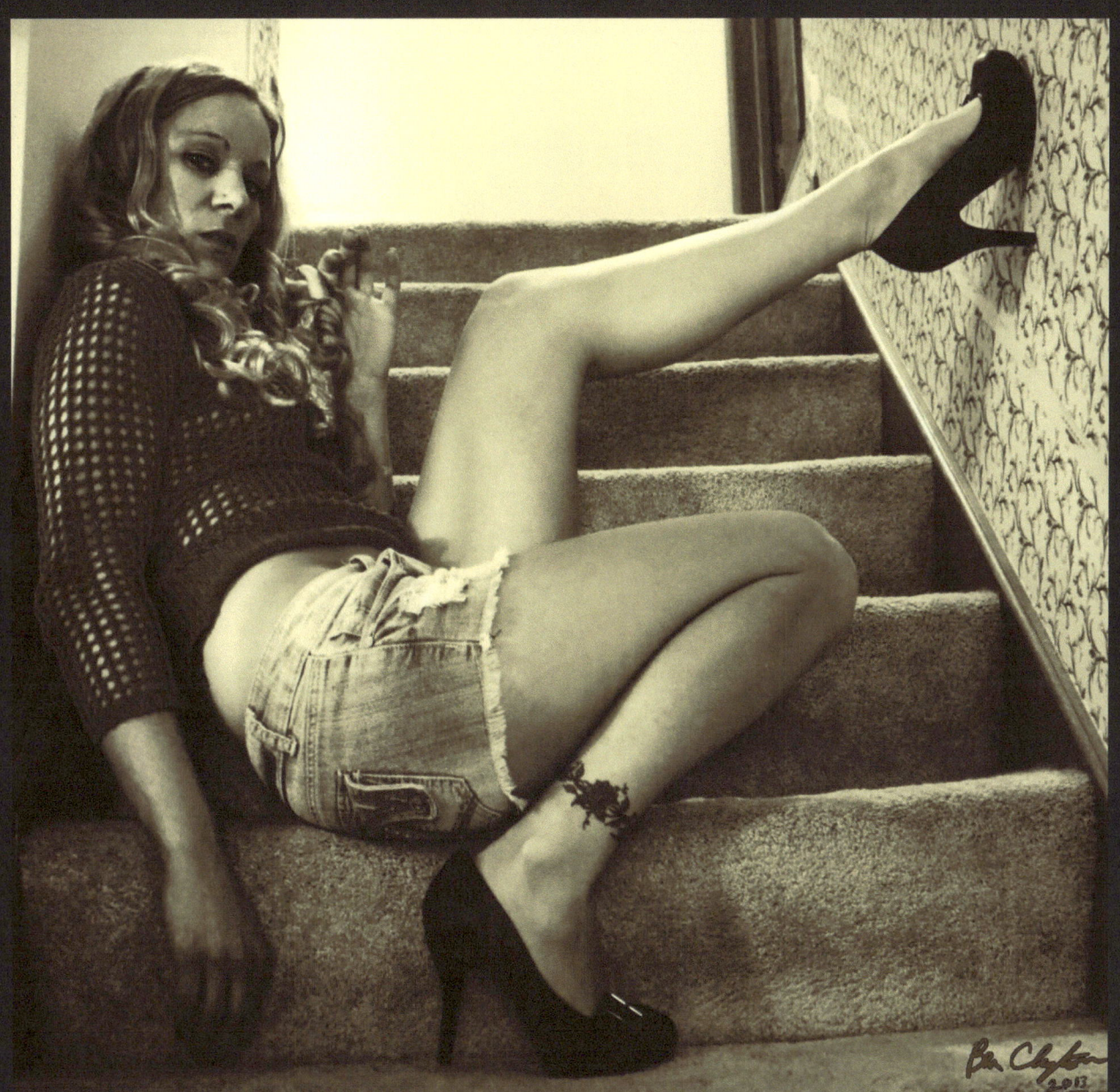

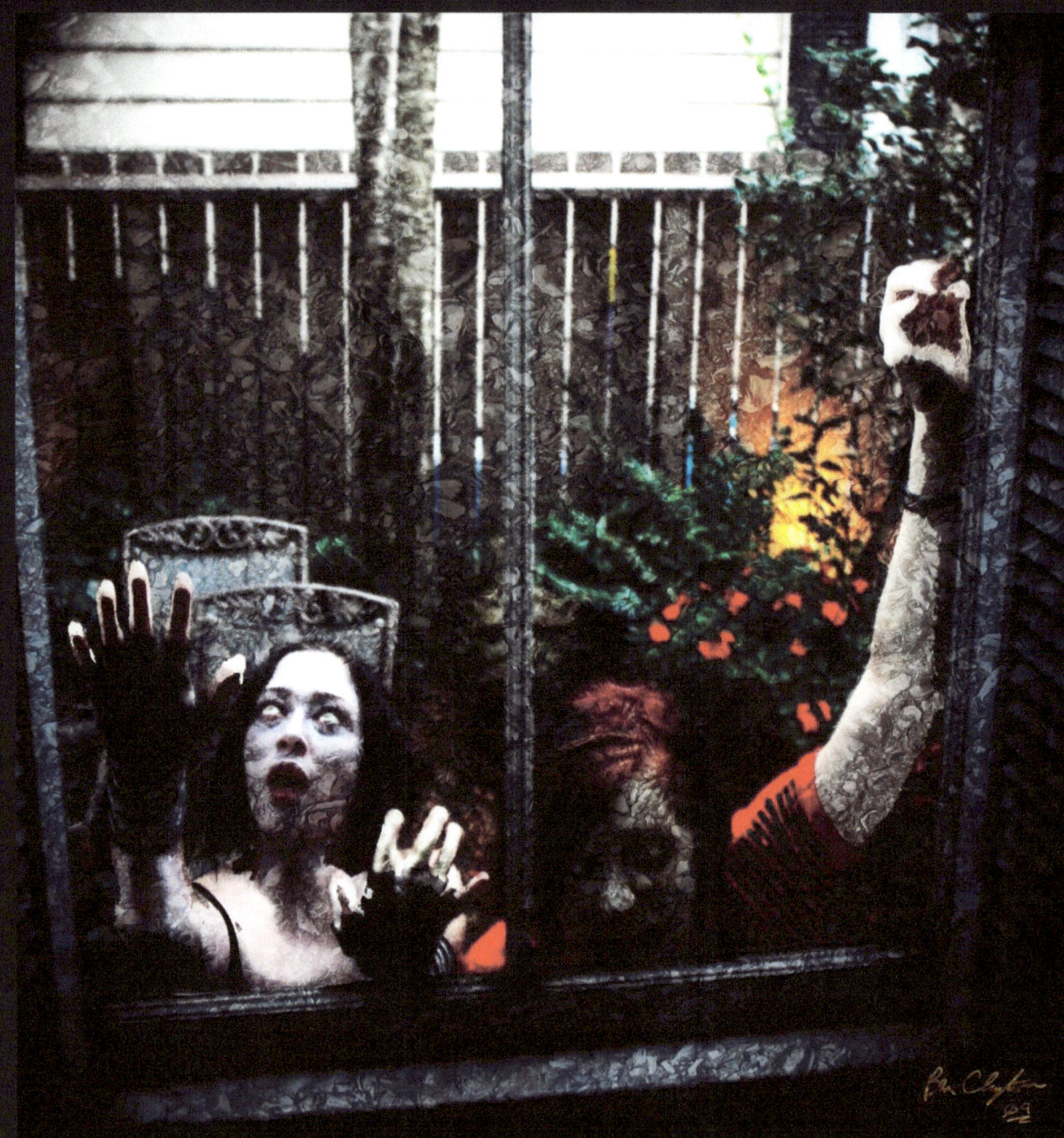

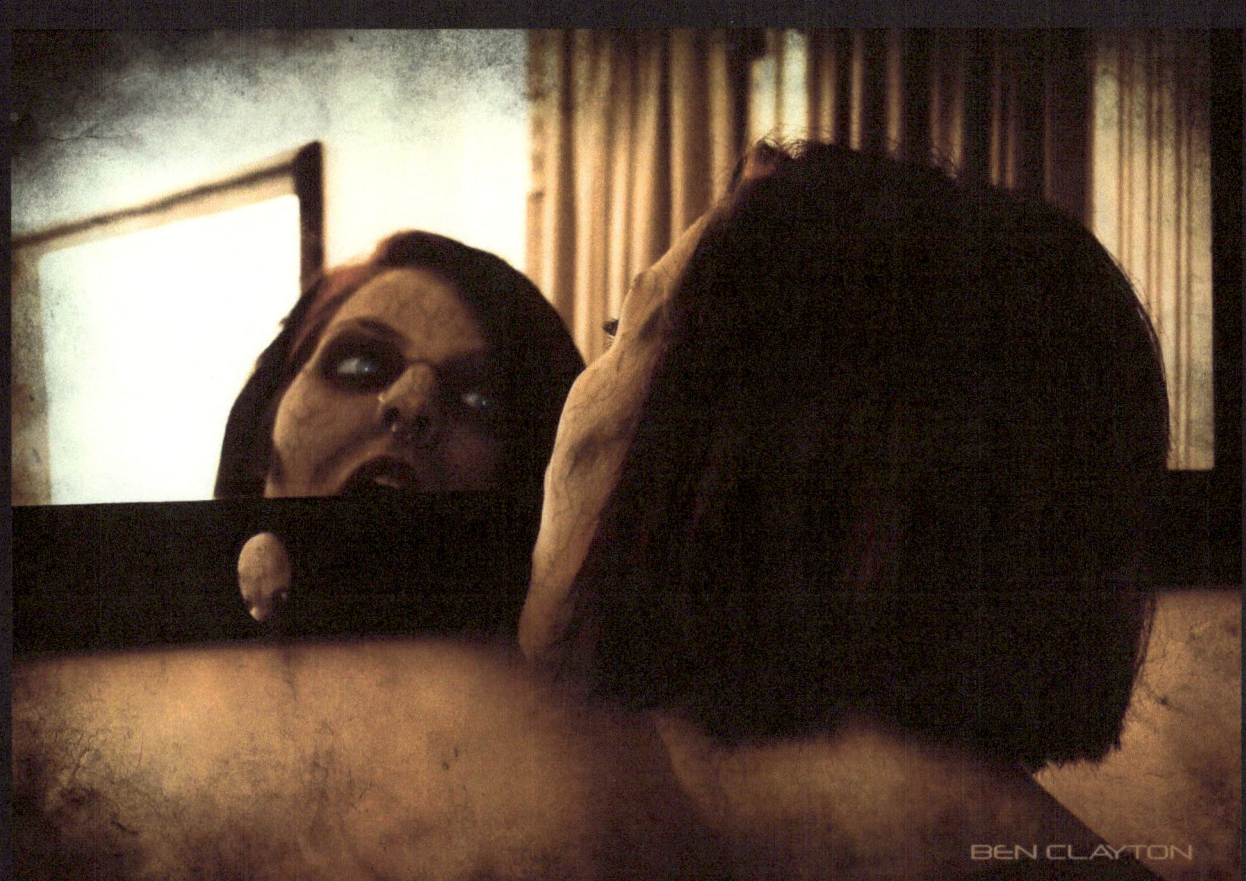

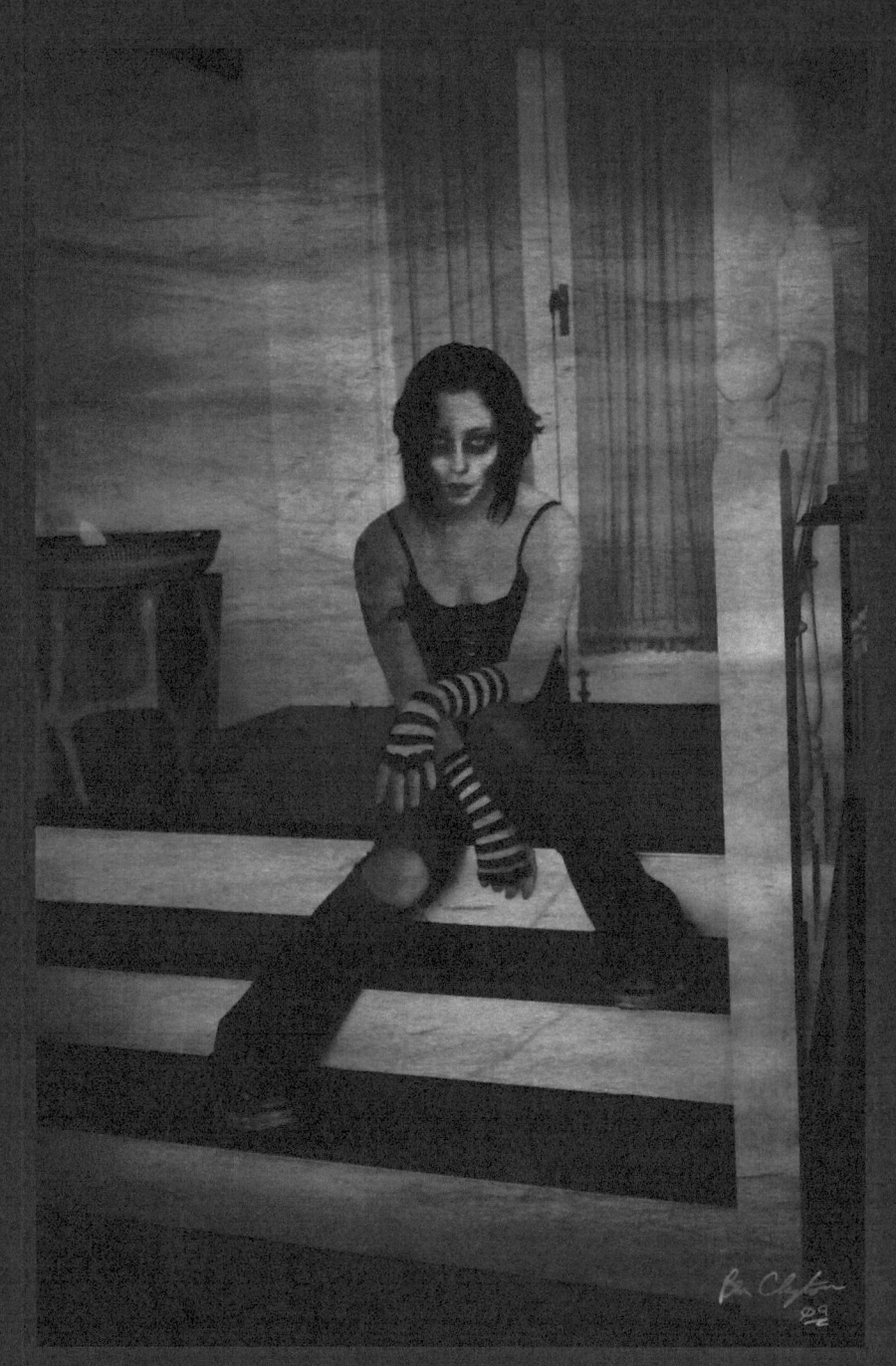

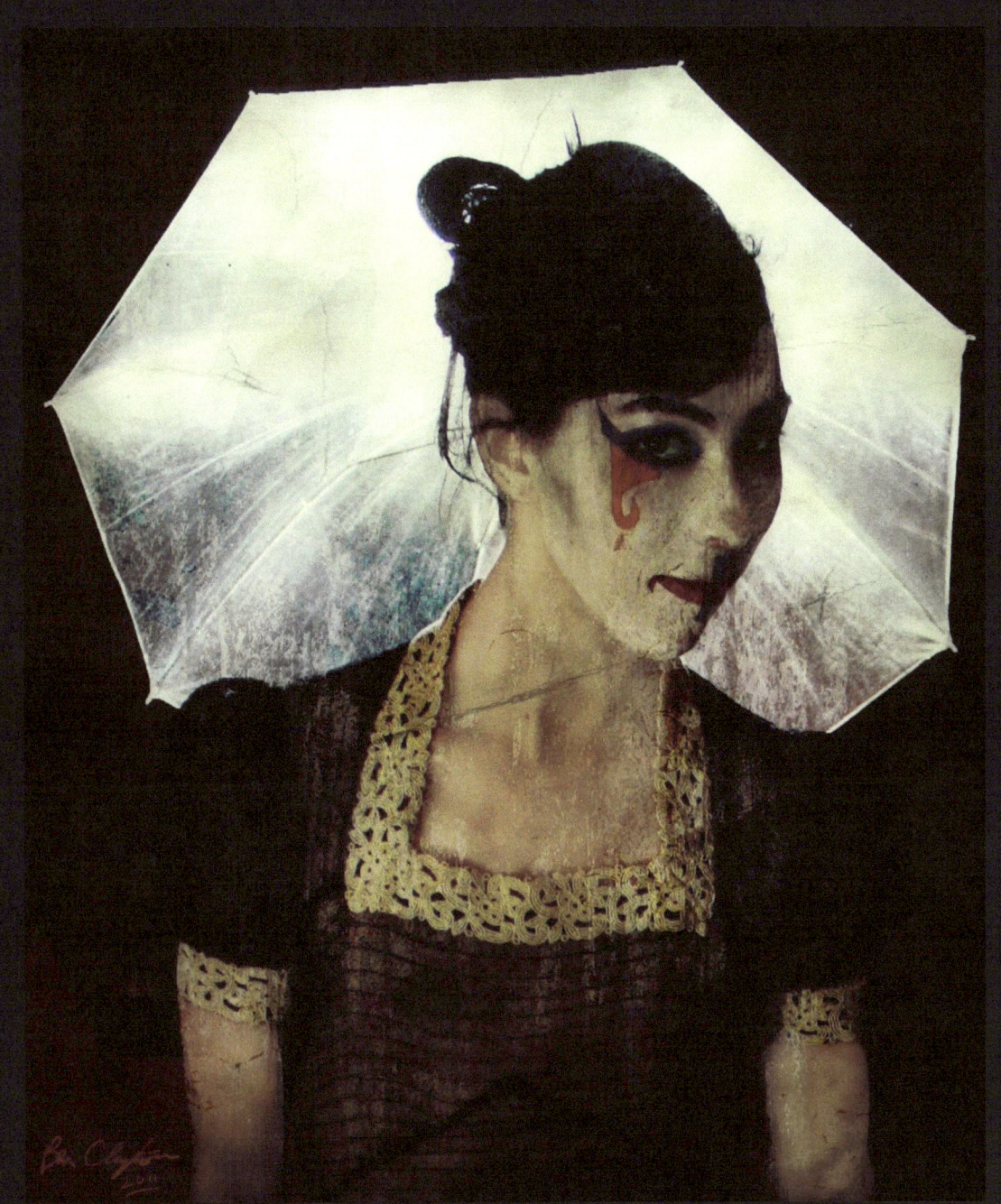

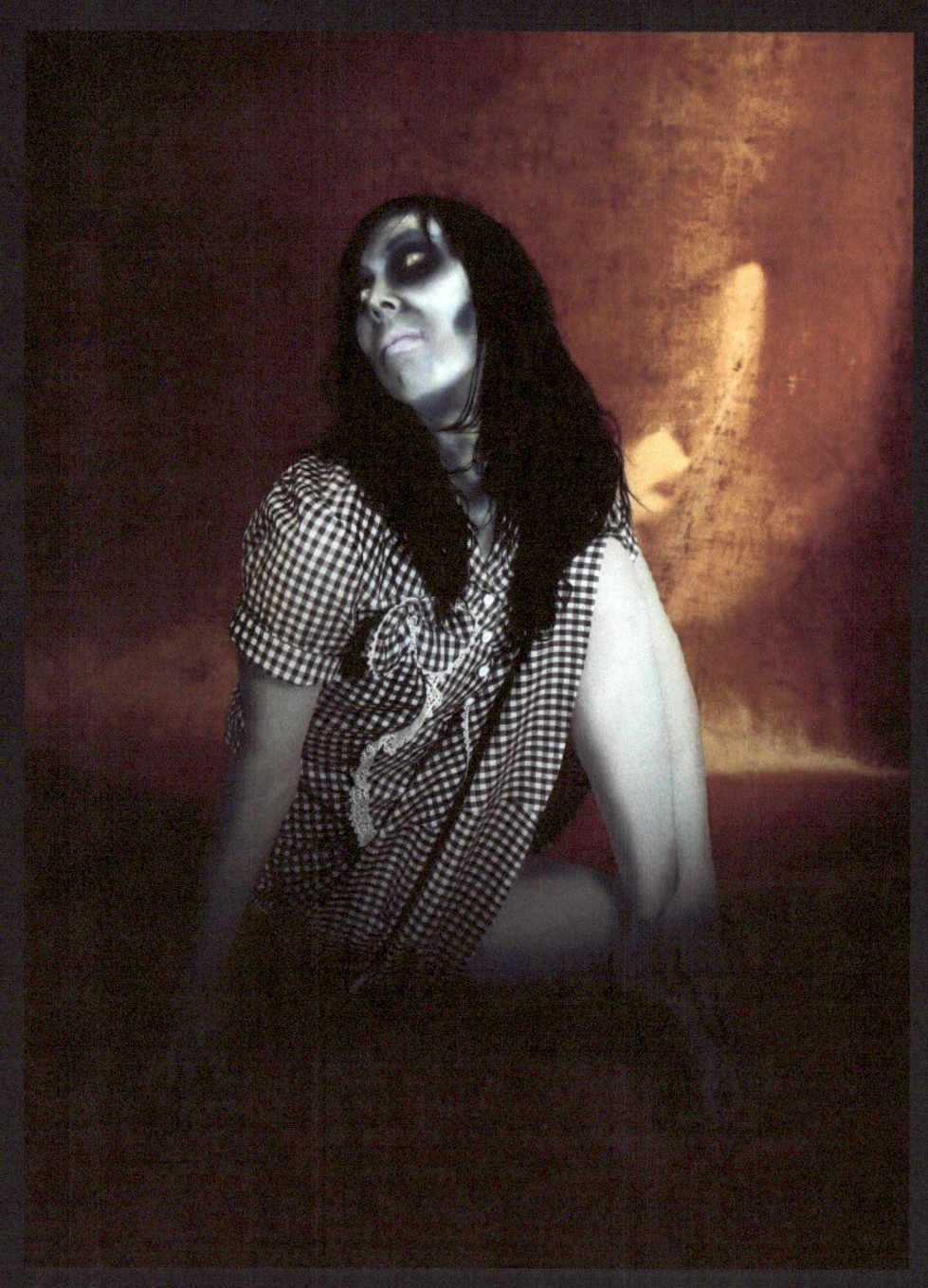

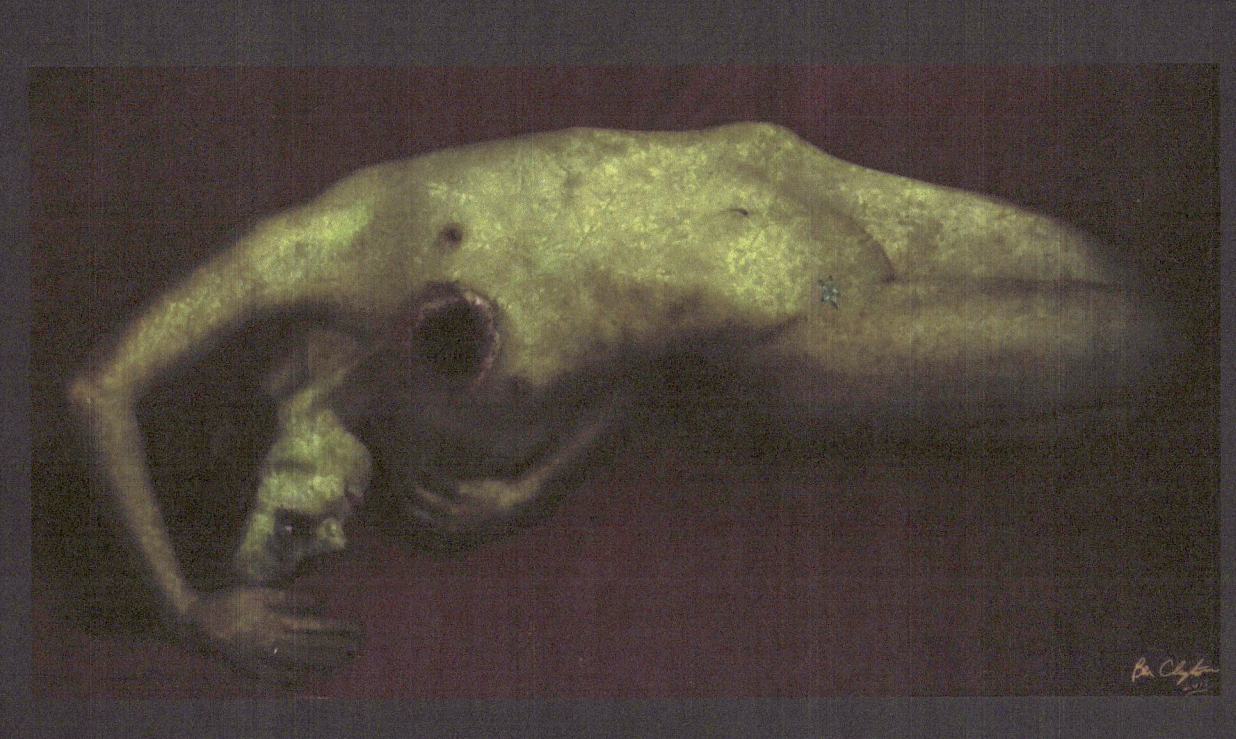

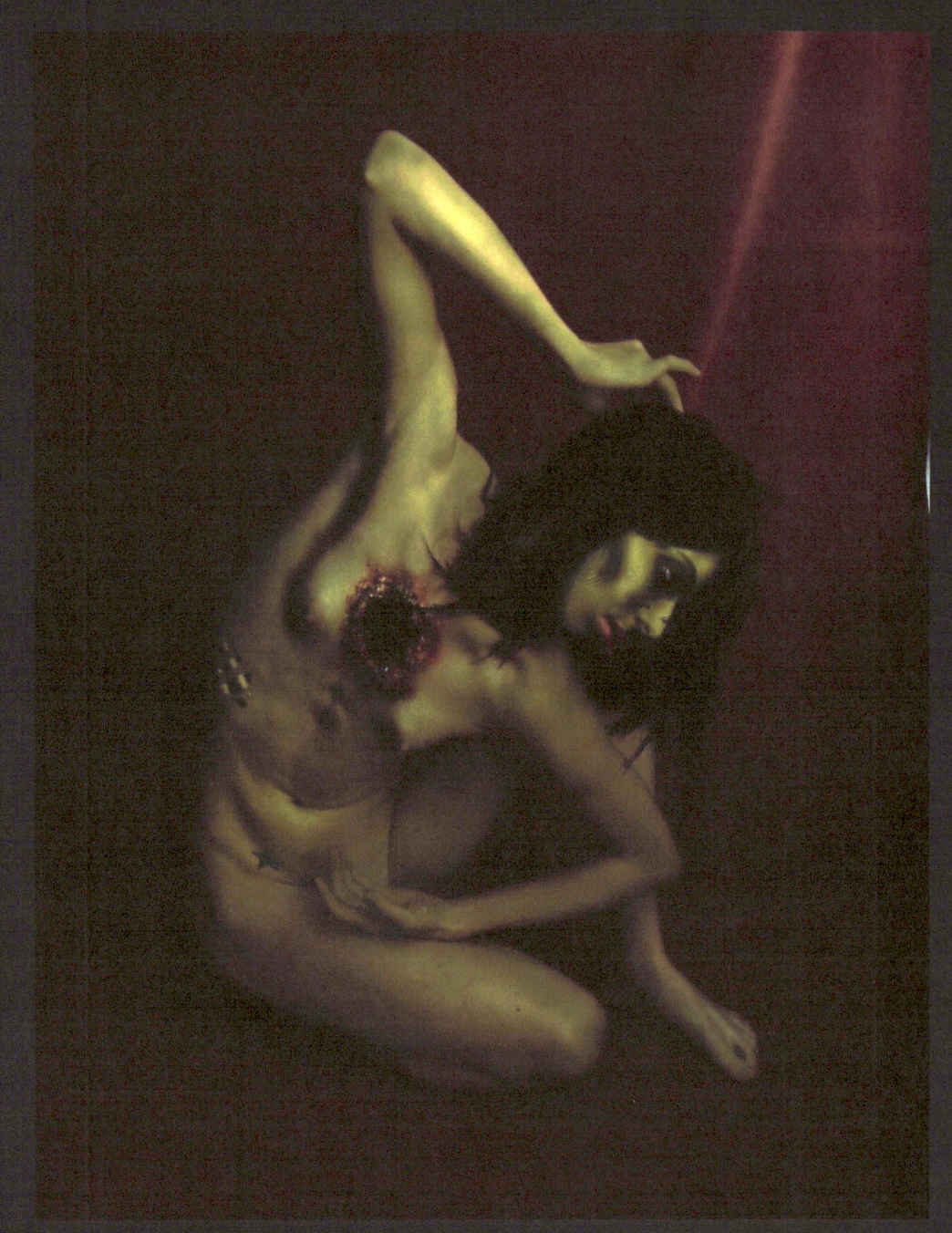

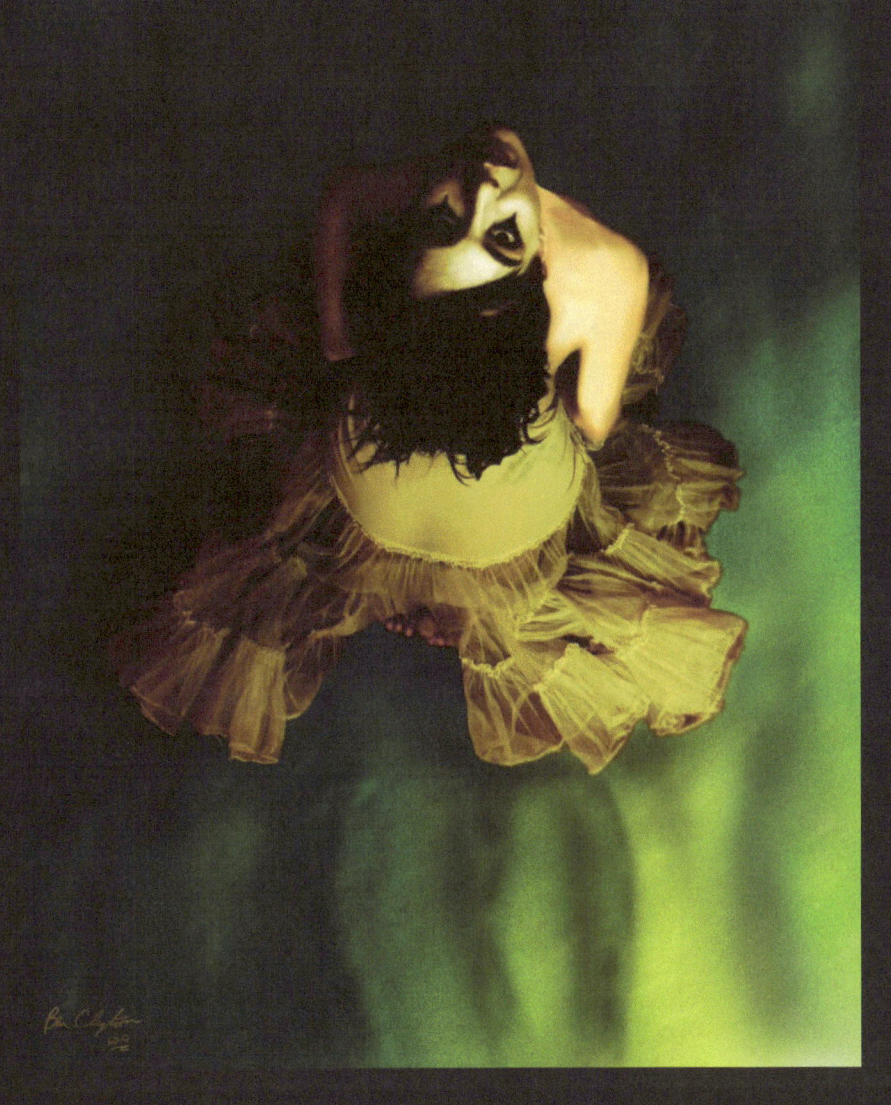

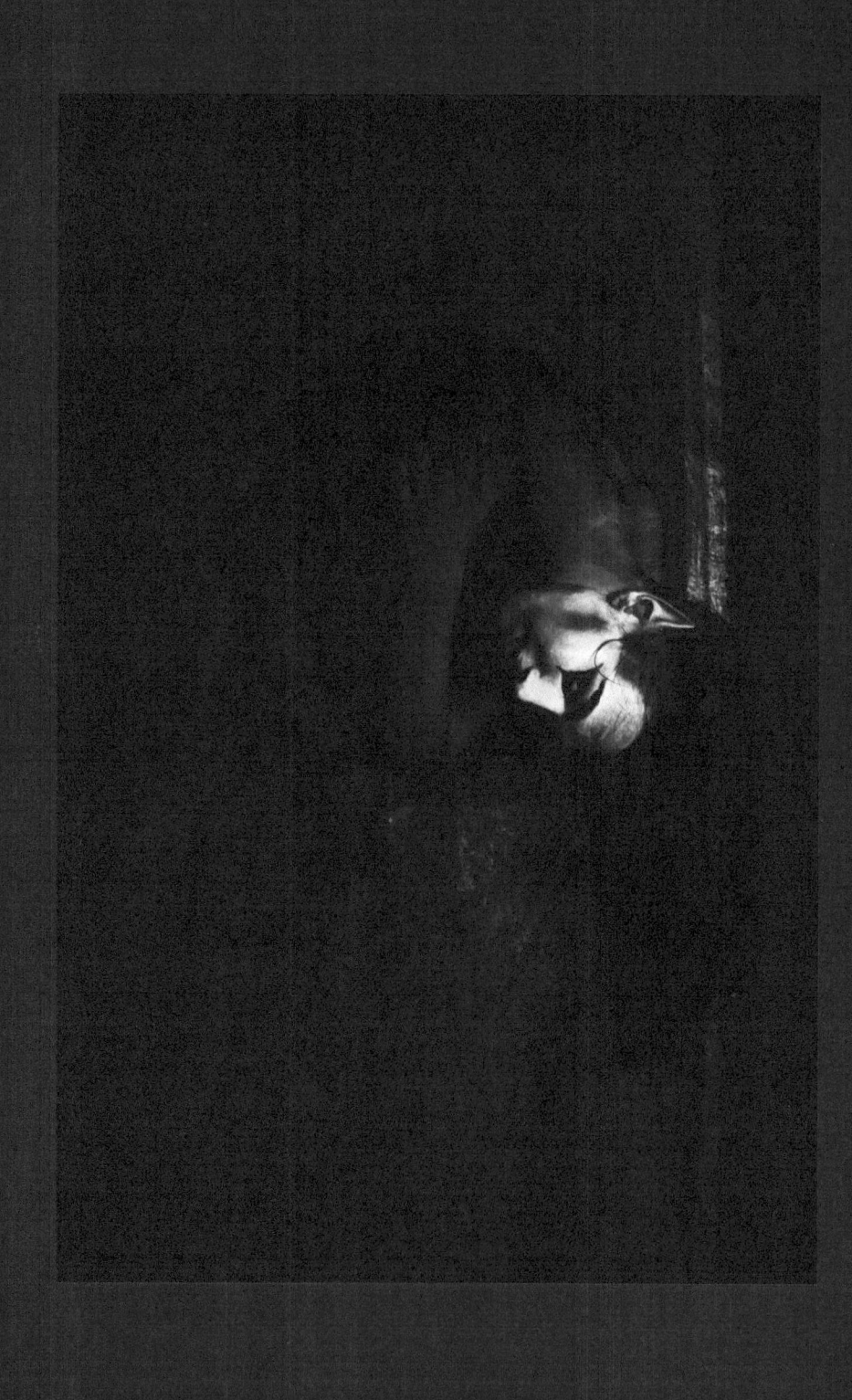

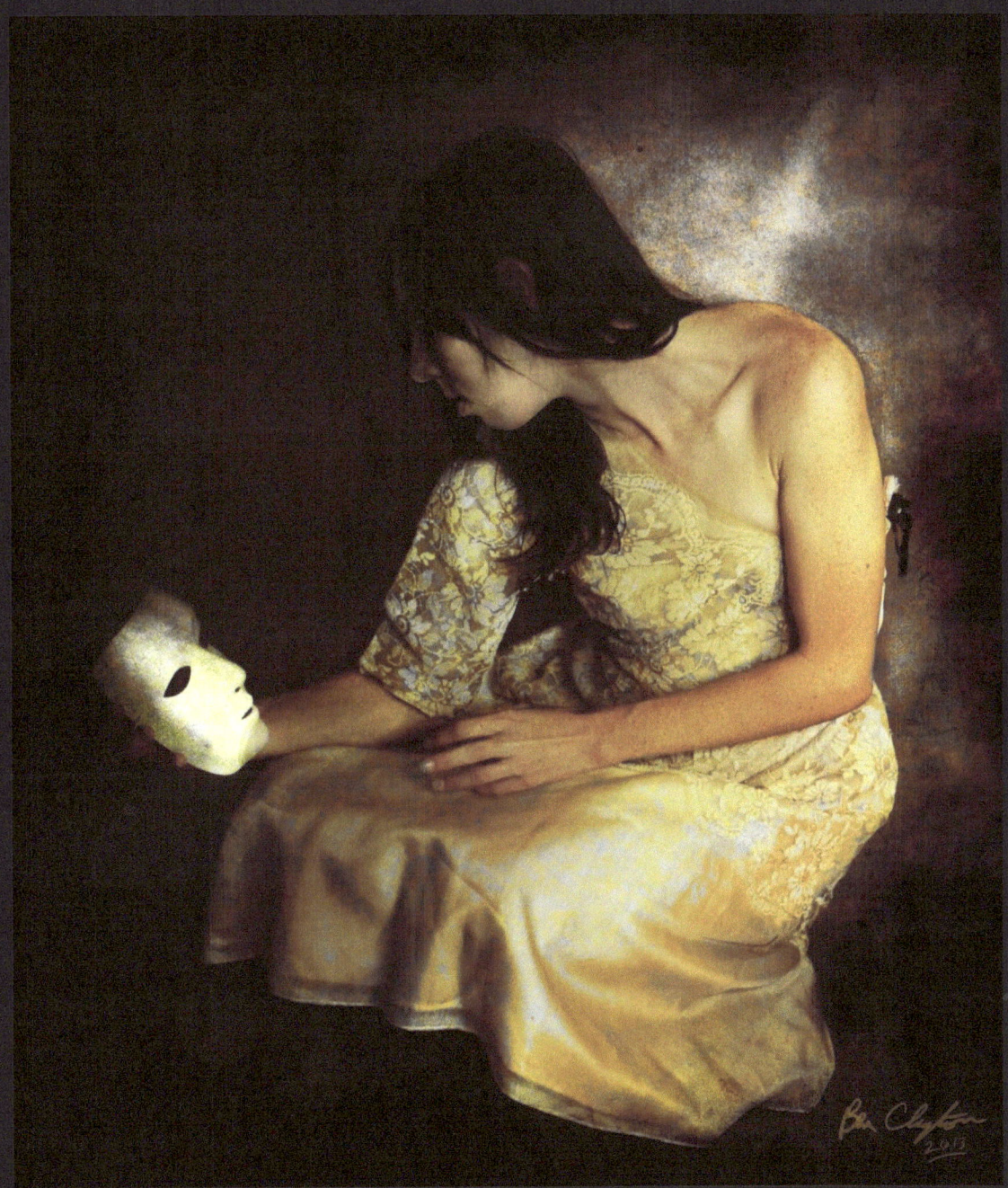

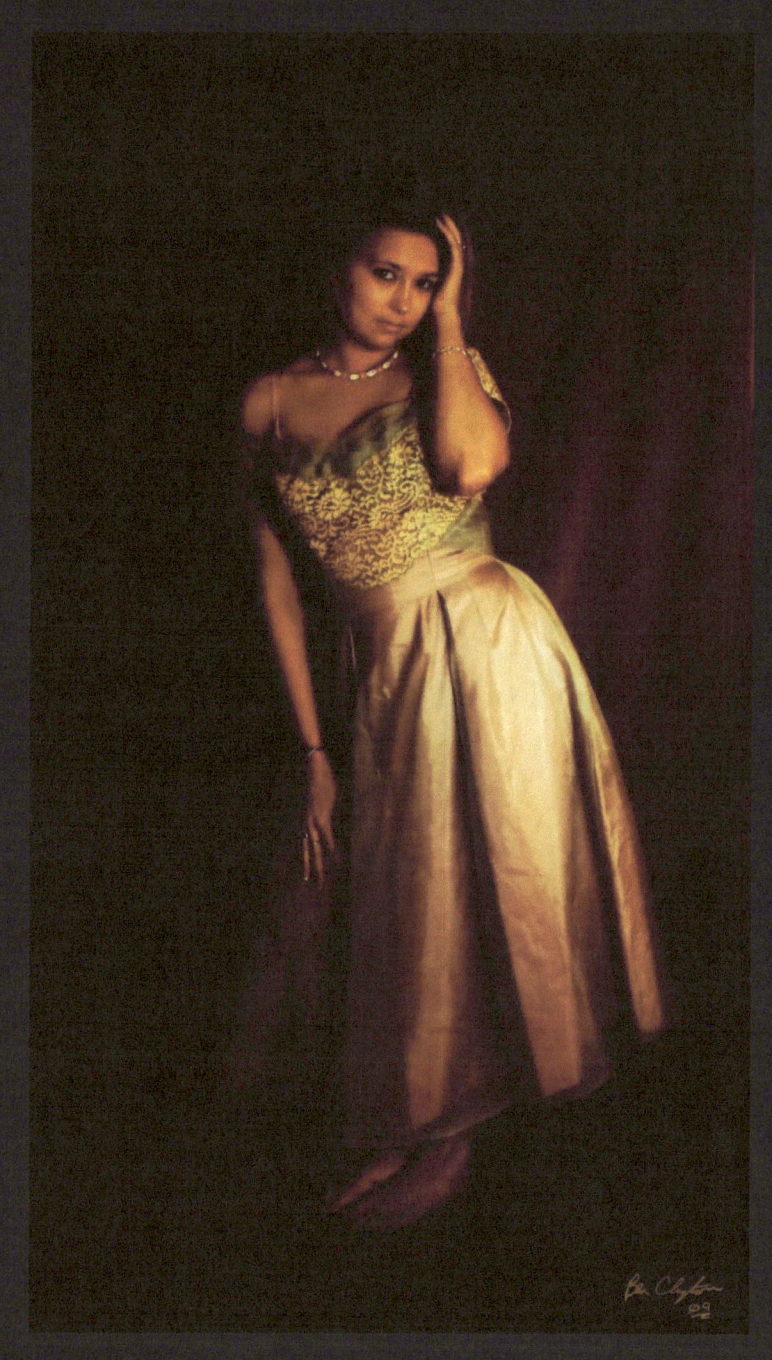

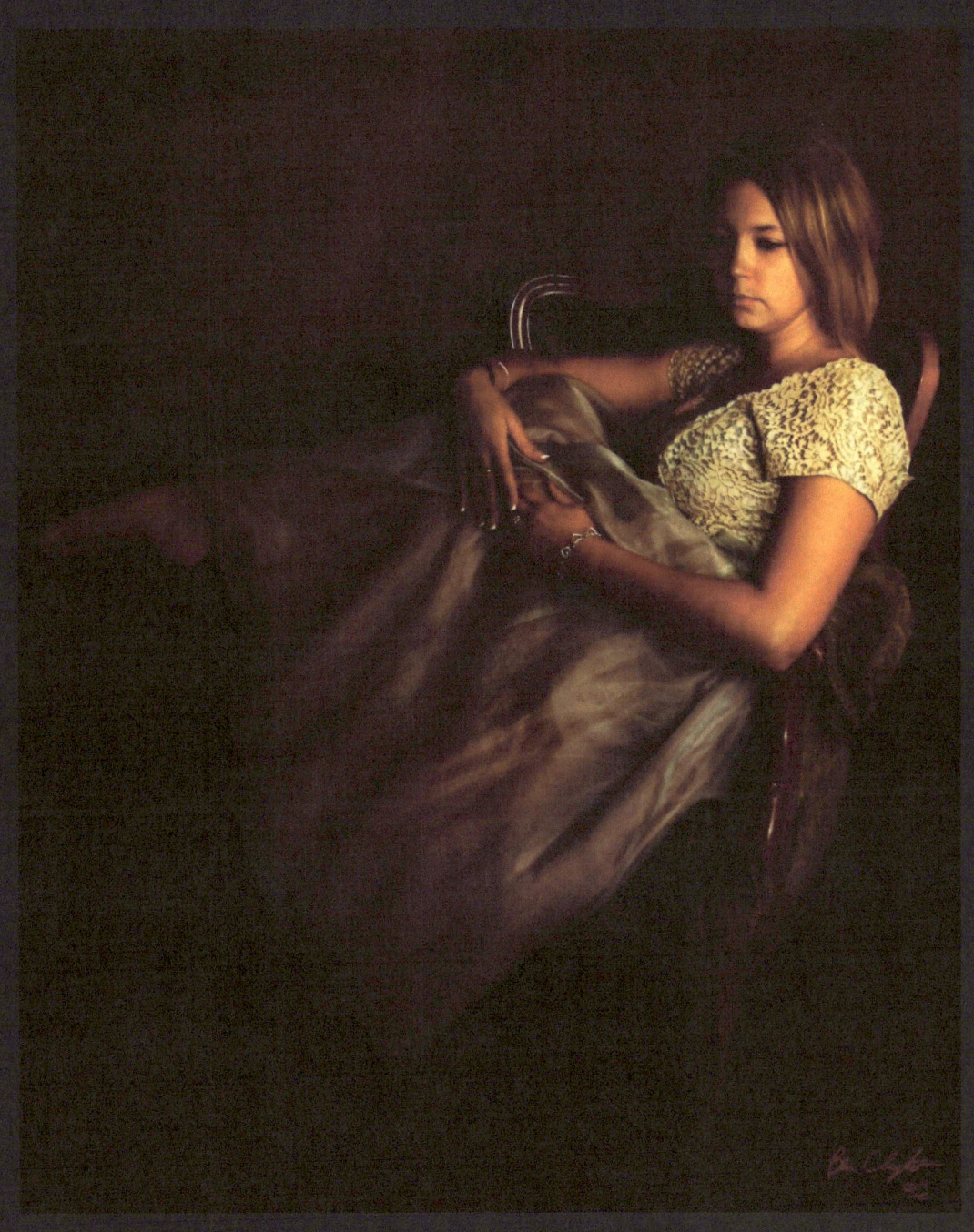

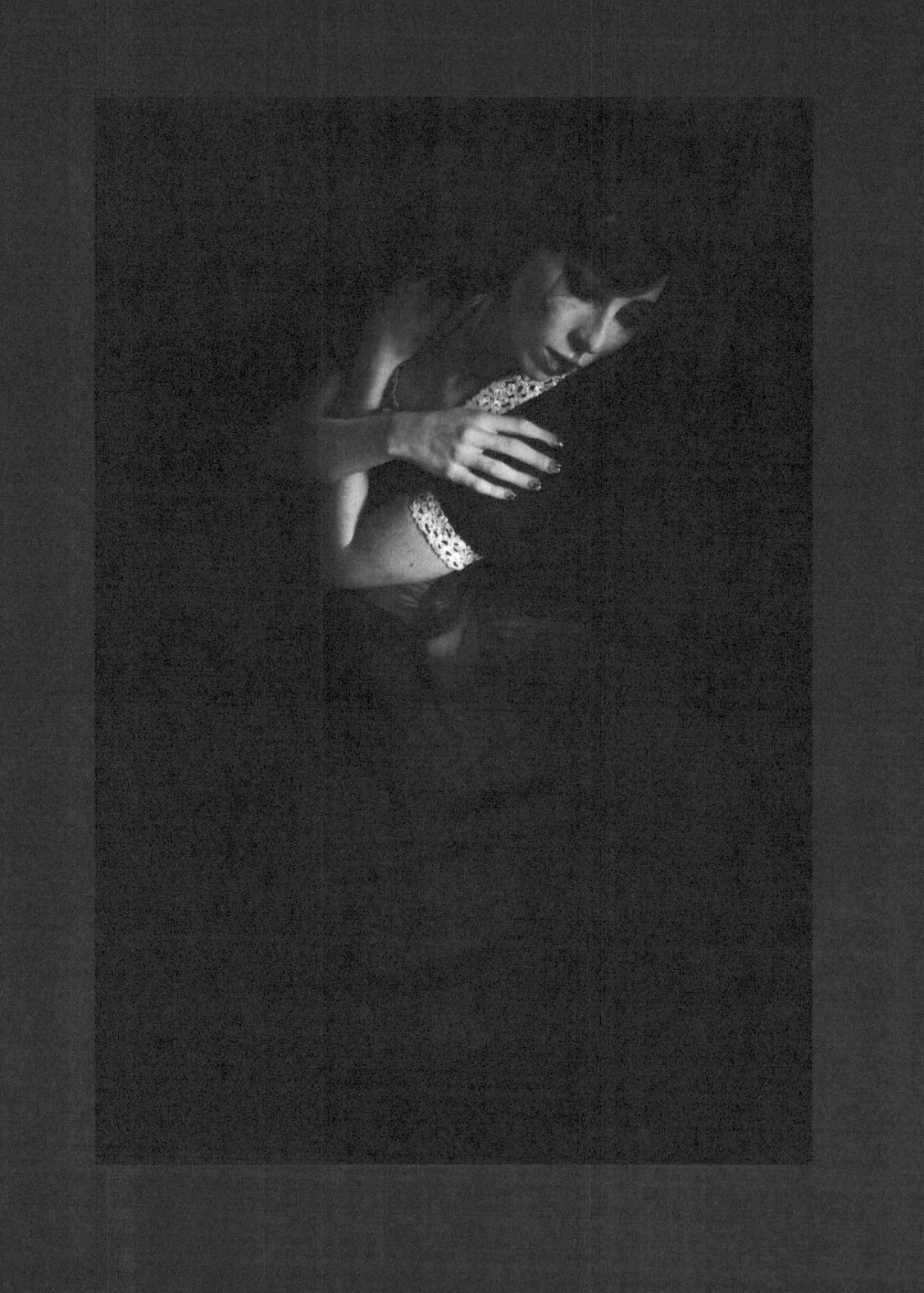

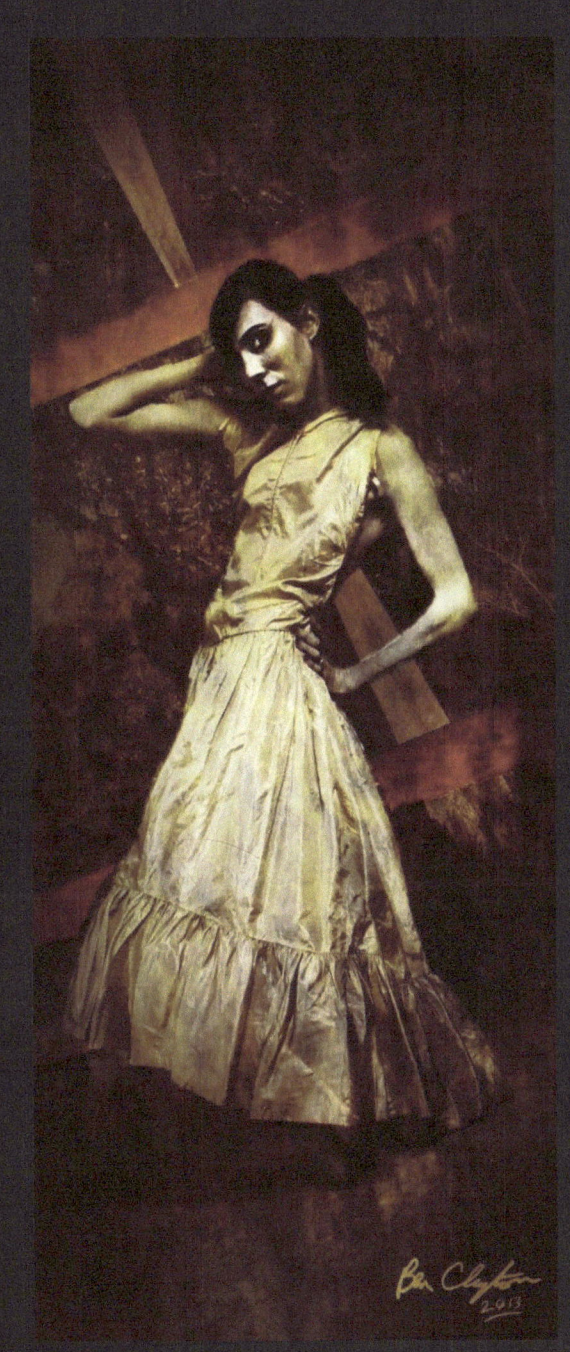

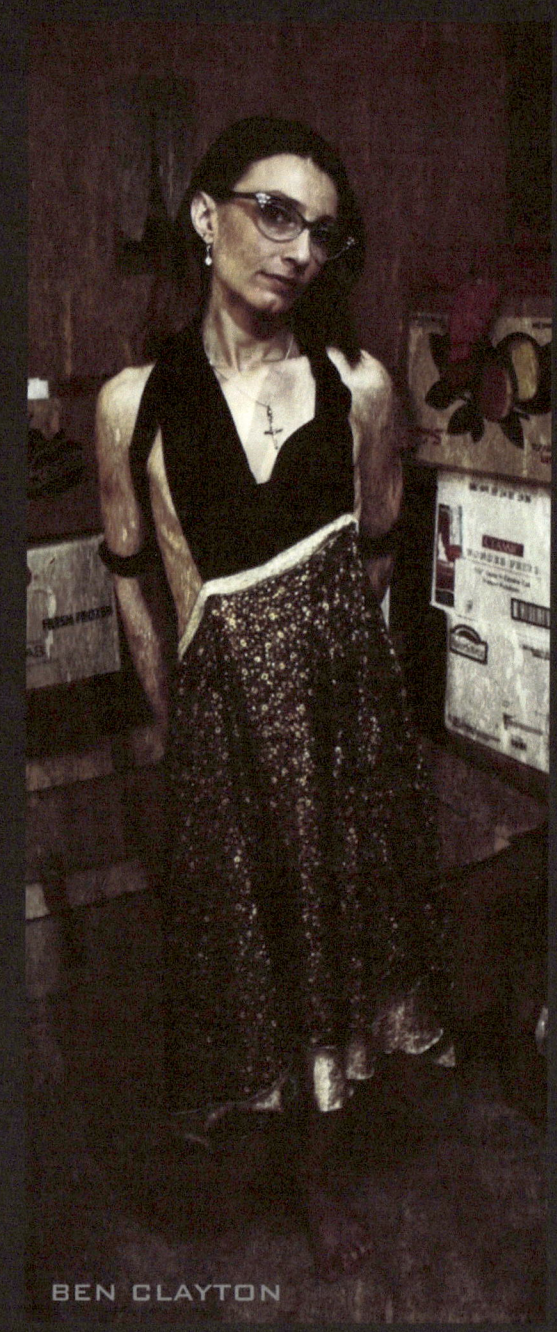

BEN CLAYTON

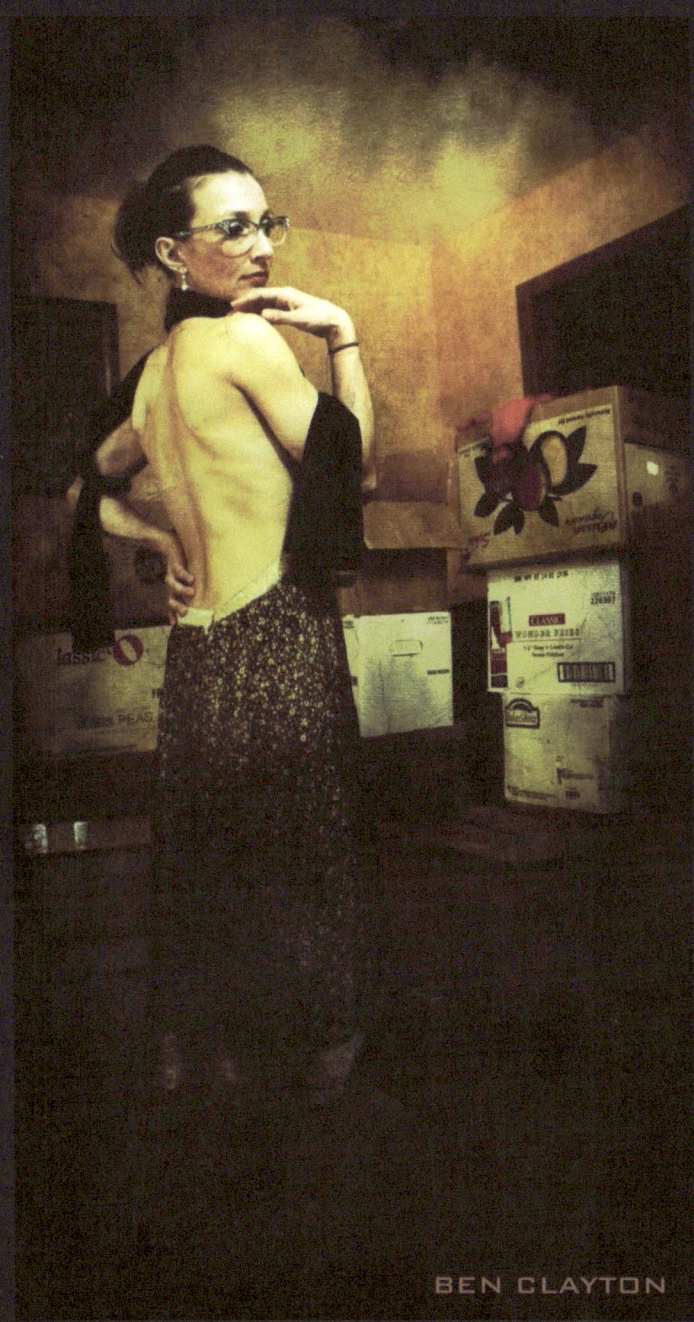

BEN CLAYTON

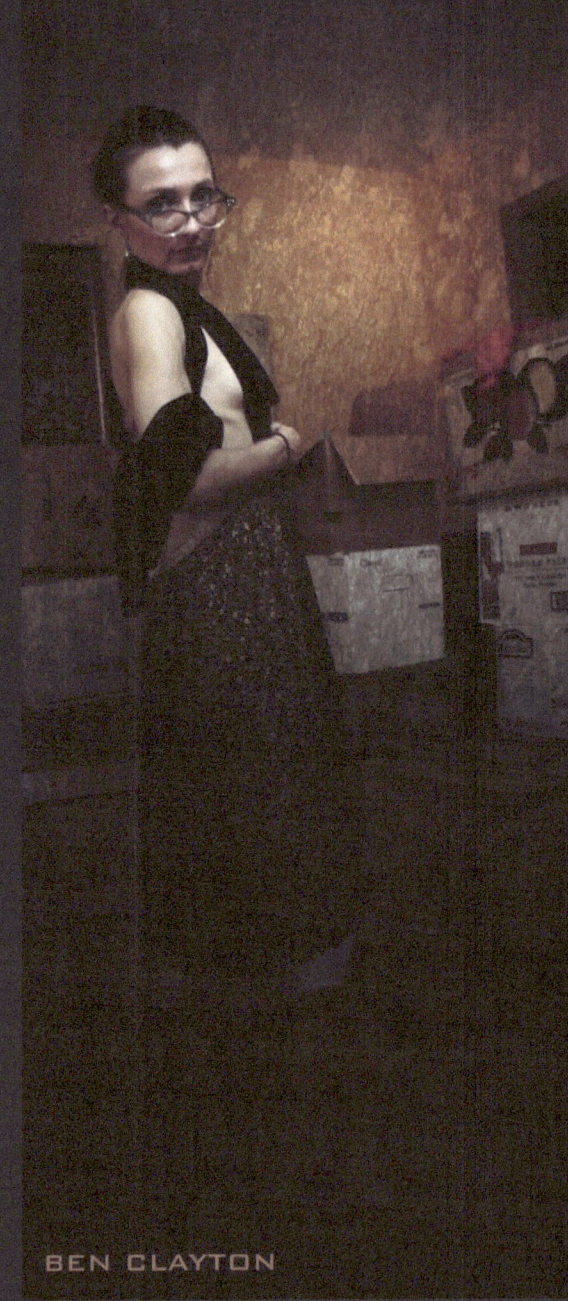

BEN CLAYTON

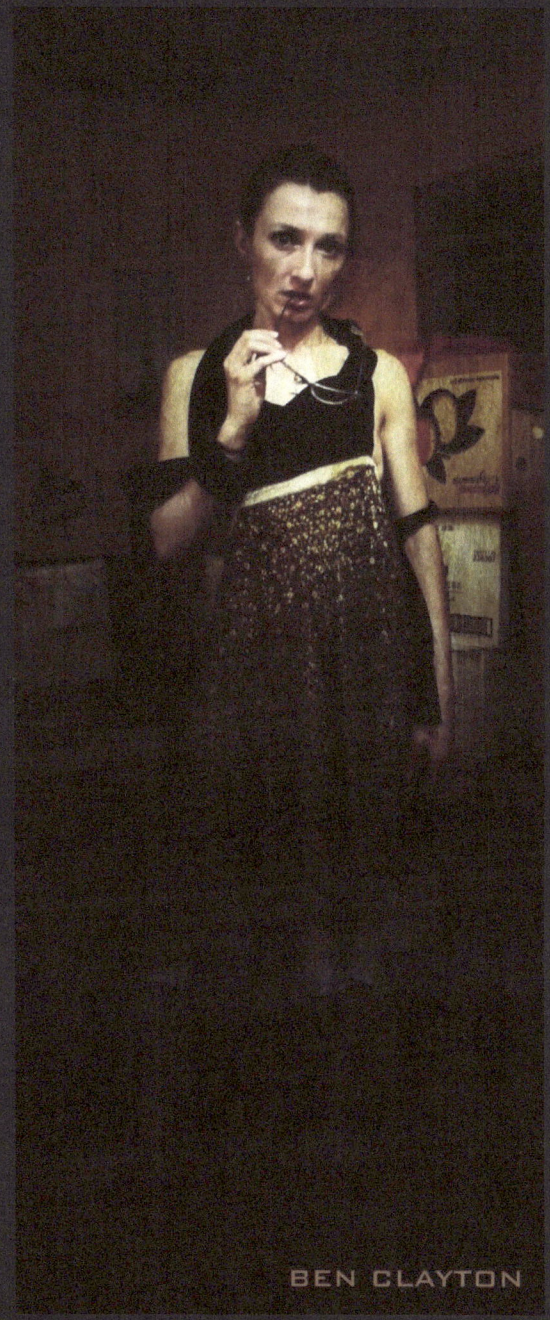

BEN CLAYTON

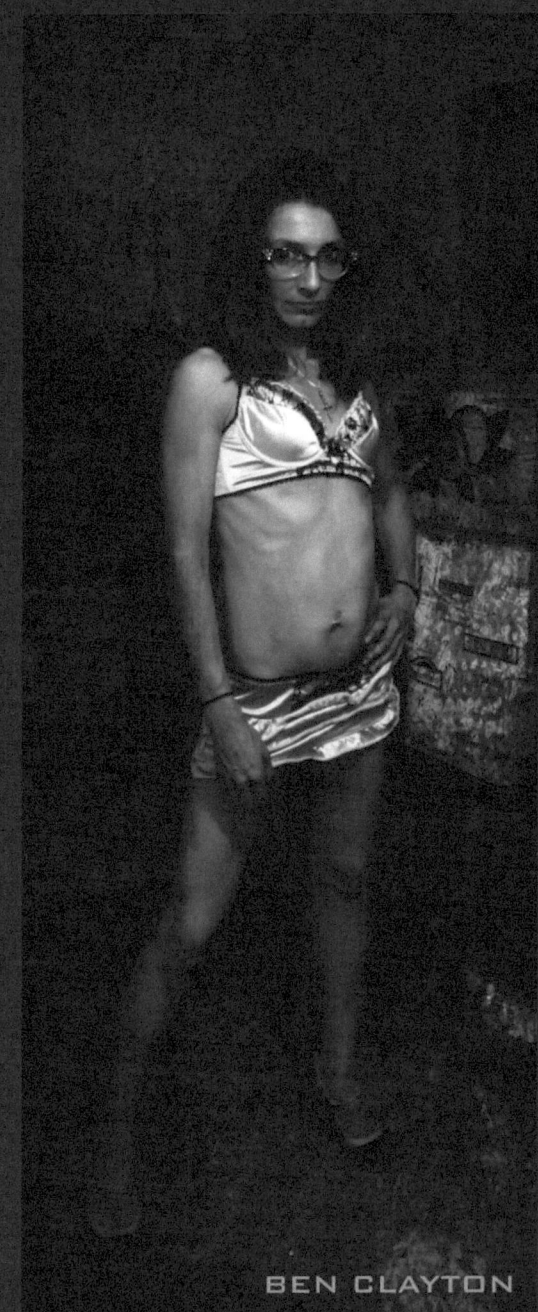
BEN CLAYTON

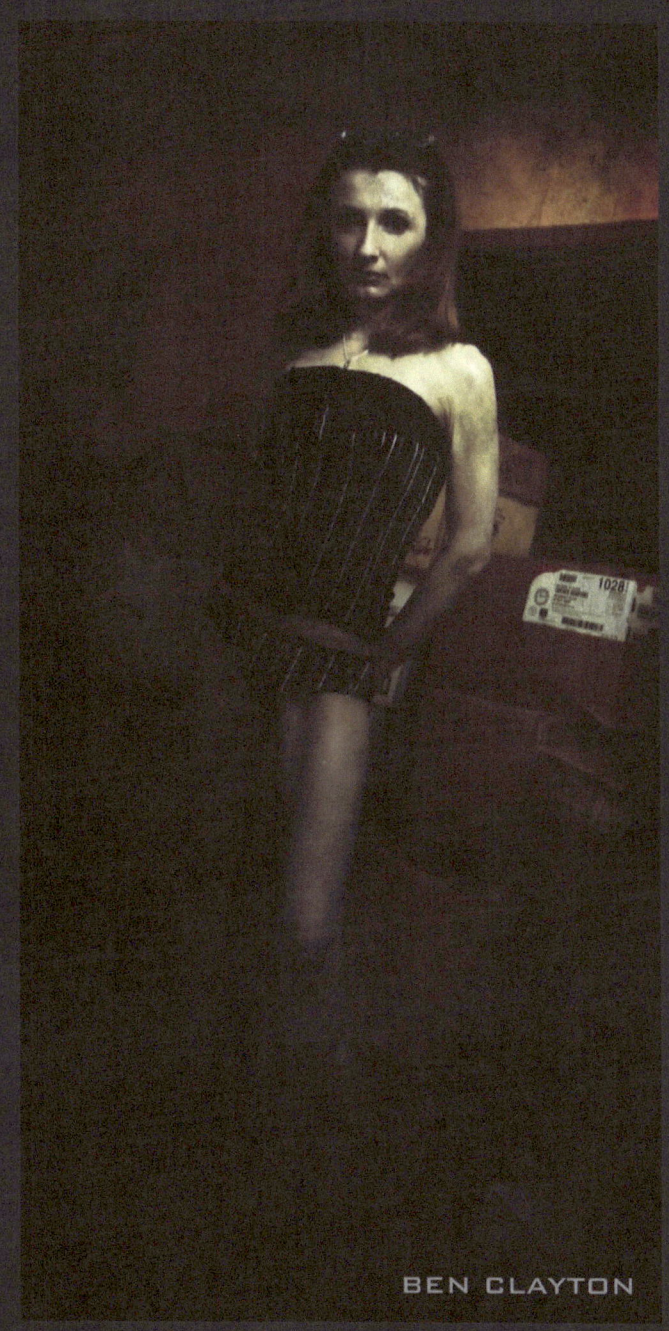

BEN CLAYTON

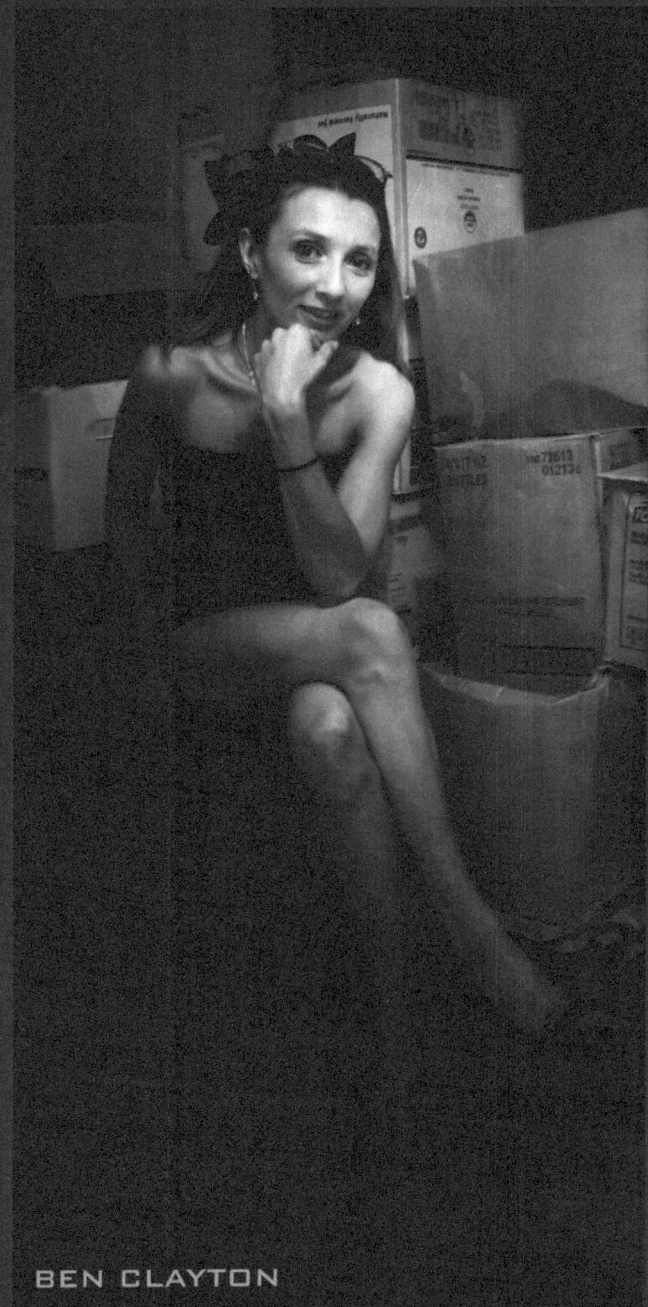

BEN CLAYTON

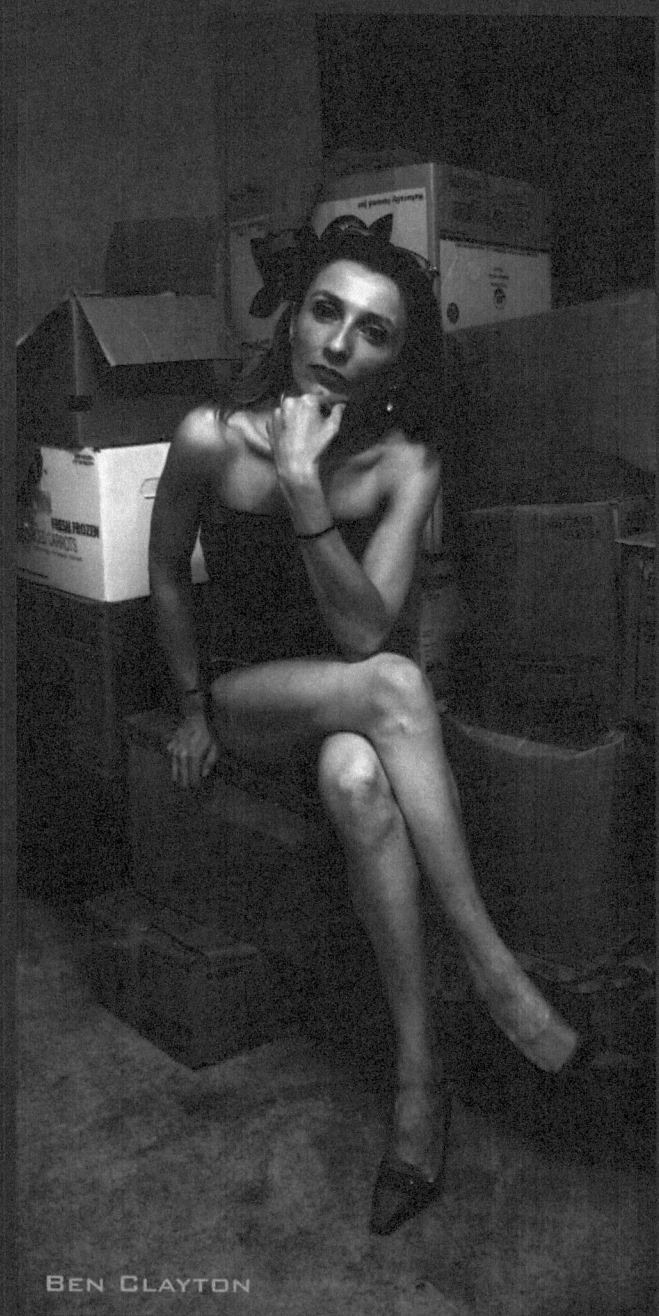

BEN CLAYTON

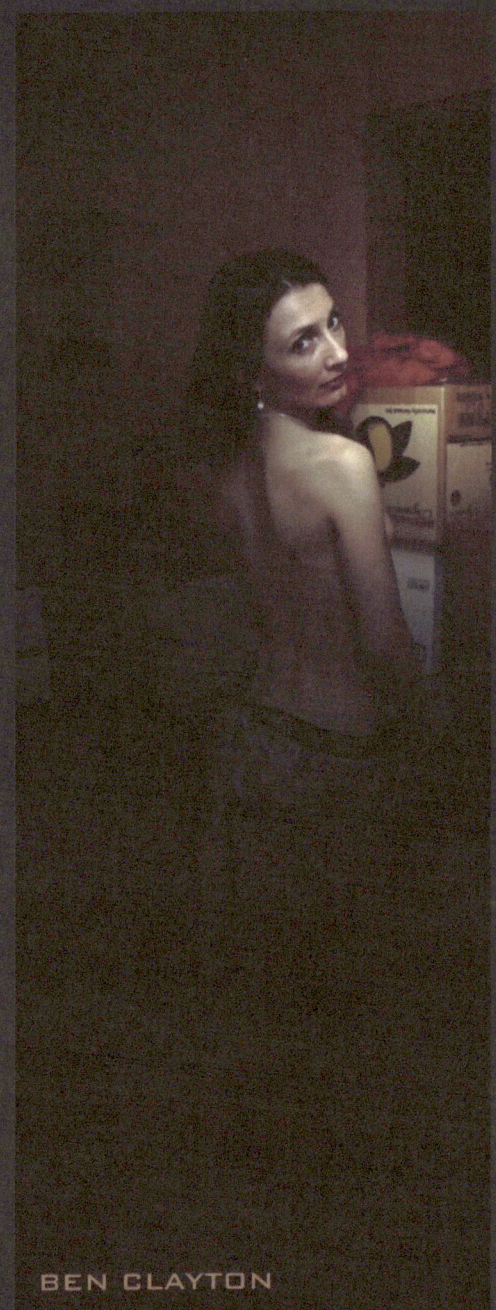

BEN CLAYTON

THANK YOU

THESE ARE THE IMAGES THAT I
ENJOY THE MOST FROM MY
COLLECTION, EXCLUDING THOSE
IN THE BOOKS
"THE LAST DAYS OF OPHELIA"
AND
"CHELSEA CHRISTIAN",
UP TO NOVEMBER 2015.
ALL IMAGES ARE AVAILABLE
INDIVIDUALLY AS PRINTS.
CONTACT LNC ART STUDIOS
FOR DETAILS.